Creating a Democratic Climate for Kids

Creating a Democratic Climate for Kids

A New Guide for Educators, Parents, and Other Significant Adults in Kids' Lives

MARY LOU MCCORMICK

ROWMAN & LITTLEFIELD
Lanham • Boulder • New York • London

Published by Rowman & Littlefield
An imprint of The Rowman & Littlefield Publishing Group, Inc.
4501 Forbes Boulevard, Suite 200, Lanham, Maryland 20706
www.rowman.com

6 Tinworth Street, London SE11 5AL, United Kingdom

Copyright © 2020 by Mary Lou McCormick

All rights reserved. No part of this book may be reproduced in any form or by any electronic or mechanical means, including information storage and retrieval systems, without written permission from the publisher, except by a reviewer who may quote passages in a review.

British Library Cataloguing in Publication Information Available

Library of Congress Cataloging-in-Publication Data

ISBN 9781475857993 (cloth)
ISBN 9781475858006 (pbk.)
ISBN 9781475858013 (electronic)

Contents

Preface ix
    A Note from the Author ix
    About Pronouns x

1 Why Methods of "The Good 'Ole Days" Are No Longer Effective in Today's Schools and Homes 1
    It Takes a Village to Raise a Child 2
    From Autocracy to Democracy 3
    The Democratic Way of Life 4
    Teaching Our Kids the Principles of Democracy 5
    Raising Good Democratic Citizens 6
    A New Age of Democratic Schools 7
    Creating A Democratic Climate in Schools and Homes 7

2 Key Concepts in the Philosophical Premises: The Power of Encouragement 11
    Rebellion and Violence Among Today's Young People 11
    All Behavior Has Social Meaning 12
    A Sense of Belonging and Social Interest 13
    The Power of Encouragement 14
    Creating New Conditions for Democratic Learning 16

3	Some Basic Counseling Tools	19
	Active Listening	20
	Reflecting the Content	21
	Reflecting Feeling	22
	Effective Inquiry	23
	Confronting	24
	Goal Setting	24
	Problem-Solving Skills	26
	Decision-Making Skills	27
	Conflict Resolution	28
	Group Resolution Strategies	33
4	Behavior Management Tips to Minimize Misbehavior	39
	A Code of Conduct with Consequences for Violations	40
	Discussion	40
	Developing a Code of Conduct	41
	Teaching the Code	42
	Enforcing the Code	43
	Reinforcement of the Code	44
	Implementing the Consequences	44
	Class Meetings	45
	Discussion	45
	The Rationale	45
	Experts Who Support the Class Meeting Concept	45
	Types of Class Meetings	46
	Benefits of Class Meetings	46
	Implementing Class Meetings	47
	Creating a Democratic Community	49
	A Peer Mediation Program	49
	Discussion	49
	Peer Mediation Models	50
	A Description of the Program	50
	Implementing the Program	51
	Peer Mediation Training Sessions	52
5	Building a Personal Democratic System of Discipline: Some Strategies, Theories and Principles to Consider	59
	Choice Theory: William Glasser	60

Discussion	61
Students' Basic Needs	61
Choice Theory Principles	61
Quality Teaching	62
Seven Deadly Habits and Seven Connecting Habits	63
Discipline with Dignity—Richard Curwin and Allen Mendler	63
Discussion	63
The Four-Phase Plan for Schools and Educators	64
Putting "Discipline with Dignity" Into Practice	65
Cooperative Discipline—Linda Albert	65
Discussion	66
Genuine and Mistaken Goals and Consequent Behaviors	66
The Three C's of Cooperation	67
Inner Discipline—Barbara Coloroso	68
Discussion	68
How Punishment Differs from Discipline	68
How to Deal with Misbehavior	68
Positive Discipline—Jane Nelson and Linda Lott	69
Discussion	70
Relationship Barriers and Relationship Builders	70
The Role of Classroom Meetings	70
The Synergetic Classroom—C. M. Charles	71
Discussion	71
Synergy and Synergetic Discipline	71
Implementing Synergetic Teaching	72
Students' Basic Needs	72
Addressing Conflicts	73
Building Your Own System of Discipline	73
What Is the Purpose of a System of Discipline?	74
Steps in Building a Discipline System	74
Involve Kids in the Process	76
Creating a Democratic Climate for Kids	76
Appendix: A Quick Reference to Useful Tools to Promote Positive Behaviors	77
Kids' Basic Needs	77
Linda Albert's Three C's for Belonging	78

Negative Ways to Get Recognition 78
A Plan for Solving Problems 79
SODAS: A Decision-Making Process 80
A Process for Setting Goals 80
Dealing with Anger/Aggression Issues 81
Helping Kids with Anger/Aggression Issues 82
Anger Analysis 83
Student Rights Regarding Bullying 84
Helping Kids Deal with Bullies 84
A Bullying/Harassment Survey 85

Bibliography 87
About the Author 93

Preface

A NOTE FROM THE AUTHOR

One of the main goals of our educational system is to teach our children the principles of democracy, yet most schools and homes are clearly run by an autocratic system, a dictatorship. Democratic principles of equality and freedom may be taught from textbooks, yet the autocratic principles of dominance-submission are still practiced in most home and school settings. It is no wonder our children feel unsettled, defiant, and even rebellious.

Civic-minded people are suddenly becoming aware that our young people are growing up ignorant of, and uncommitted to, the great principles upon which our nation was founded. The simple truth of the matter is that our young people are not committed to democratic principles, political freedom, or the Bill of Rights because they do not experience any of these matters in their everyday life and, in particular, in their schools and homes.

The way to make children committed to our American democratic way of life is to make them full participants in it. If we make our schools and homes models of democracy, give our kids the freedom of choice, and bestow on them the basic rights of citizenship, they will have no trouble understanding what our country is about.

This practical handbook will assist educators—teachers, counselors, administrators, and other school staff members—as well as parents and guardians, in creating a democratic climate for kids by developing new strategies and skills based on democratic principles as they stimulate today's kids into becoming self-reliant, self-disciplined, and self-managing individuals, a gift that will last a lifetime.

ABOUT PRONOUNS

It is not easy in the English language to refer to a child without indicating whether the child is a "he" or "she." To resolve this difficulty, I have chosen to alternate the usage of the pronouns, although reference may be made to either sex. Please imagine that the child being referred to is the child you have in mind, even though the sex reference may not agree.

1

Why Methods of the "Good Ole Days" Are No Longer Effective in Today's Schools and Homes

The democratic principles of equality and freedom are taught from the textbooks, yet the autocratic principles of dominance-submission and superiority-inferiority are still practiced in many actual home and school settings.

It is a tough business being a parent, educator, or counselor in today's world. At times, we have all felt confused, bewildered, frustrated, and even harassed by our kids. Underneath it all is the fact that we often do not know what to do with our kids because we lack new methods based on democratic principles with which to guide and educate them into democratic social living.

All cultures and civilizations develop a definite plan for raising and educating their children. Each culture has its own procedures and policies with which to meet life problems, situations, and challenges. Throughout history in our own country, every man, woman, and child knew exactly what was expected of them. Behavior was established by tradition.

Attitudes of today's children are quite different from what they were back in "the good ole days." Many of our young people no longer accept parents' and teachers' judgments as absolute. Defiance and even outright rebellion are becoming more and more characteristic of even very young children.

Fair and reasonable rules give children a sense of security, a feeling they belong to the group; they let kids know what kind of behavior is expected of them. Kids are far more likely to follow the rules and abide by the consequences of breaking the rules if they have played an active role in creating them. In a democratic society, we have a voice in making the laws by which we are expected to live, and so should kids have a voice in making the rules that guide them in the home and school settings. Clearly, most of our schools and homes are not democratic places for kids.

The principles of democracy, freedom, and the rights of individuals are taught from the textbooks, but the principles of autocracy and dictatorship are still practiced in most of our schools and homes. Principals, teachers, and other educators, as well as parents, guardians, and other significant adults in kids' lives, must assume their roles as democratic leaders for our children in today's society, or we just might risk losing our democratic way of life as we know it.

IT TAKES A VILLAGE TO RAISE A CHILD

Parents and teachers have covered up for kids, endured their insults, put up with their many demands, and consequently, many have lost their influence and control over them. In the so-called "good ole days," most parents unquestionably supported the judgments of teachers and administrators.

In this day and age, we are seeing almost a schism between the school and the home. Parents blame the school system for their children's defiant, rebellious, and underachieving behavior. The school system blames the parents for their students' disobedient conduct, their apathetic attitude toward school and learning, and their general disregard for authority.

Teachers are finding it increasingly more challenging to communicate with parents, and parents are having greater difficulty relating their concerns to teachers. The two most important sets of adults in a child's life—his parents and his teachers—are not communicating effectively, and the child is either caught in the middle or falls through the cracks.

Add to this already grim scenario the fact that many teachers have an increasingly larger number of students in their classes, and more and more children live in single-parent homes or have both parents working outside of the home. This allows teachers even less time to meet the intellectual and academic needs of individual students and affords parents and guardians less time to meet the emotional, personal, and social needs of their children.

In today's world the phrase "It takes a village to raise a child" has taken on new meaning. Indeed, it takes *both* the home *and* the school, working together to effectively meet the emotional, personal, social, intellectual, and academic needs of a child in today's society.

FROM AUTOCRACY TO DEMOCRACY

Our developing awareness of the meaning of democracy and its effects upon interpersonal relationships has profoundly changed our culture. From the time of the kings and serfs up to the present, mankind has gradually come to realize that man is created equal, not just in the eyes of the law, but equal in the sight of his fellow men and women. The implication of this awareness is that democracy is not just a political ideal but also a way of life.

The cries for equality and justice ring out across our nation. Women are no longer satisfied with being treated as second-class citizens; they want "equal pay for equal work." They want equal rights!

African Americans, Hispanics, Native Americans, Asians, and other ethnic and racial minorities refuse to "stay in their place" as inferior beings. They want equal rights!

The gay population is no longer willing to hide under the social carpet of society and stay "out of sight, out of mind," or as they used to say in the military, "don't ask, don't tell," for fear of negative repercussions. They want equal rights!

More and more teenagers and even young children report their parents or guardians to the police and to child protective services for what they perceive as unfair wrongdoing toward them. They sense unjust treatment.

Many parents, educators, and other significant adults in kids' lives get deeply disturbed at the notion that children are their equals. Just as in the larger society, equality is not based on experience, abilities, or skills. Equality means that *all* people have equal claims to dignity, respect, and fair treatment, *despite* all their individual differences and abilities. This means children also have the right to be treated with dignity, respect, and fairness.

Dinkmeyer and Dreikurs (1963) emphasized that it is largely the impact of democracy that has transformed our social atmosphere and has made the traditional methods of disciplining children obsolete. We no longer have rulers such as those who prevailed in the autocratic society from which we have recently emerged, historically speaking.

In a democratic society of equals, we cannot dominate or rule over others. We have personal rights and freedoms. But where is the democracy in most of our schools and homes? They are generally not democratic places for children.

One of the main goals of our educational system is to teach our children the principles of democracy, yet most schools are clearly run by an autocratic system, a dictatorship. Democratic principles of equality and freedom may be taught from textbooks, yet the autocratic principles of dominance-submission and superiority-inferiority are still practiced in most home and school settings. It is no wonder our children feel unsettled, defiant, and even rebellious.

THE DEMOCRATIC WAY OF LIFE
This change in our social atmosphere from the autocratic relationship of dominance and submission to the democratic relationship of equals has brought about widespread confusion about how to apply these principles to our homes and schools.

To many, democracy means freedom to do as one pleases. Many of our young people have reached the point where they rebel against rules and restrictions because they assume their right to do as they please. They see these rules and restrictions as a form of adult control that has been imposed upon them. But this is not freedom. Just as in our larger society, if everyone insisted on doing as he or she pleased, there would be total chaos with resulting anarchy. Stress, strain, and friction would result, producing tension, anger, and hostility—all negative aspects of social living.

Undeniably, freedom is part of democracy, but the point is that we cannot have freedom unless we respect the freedom and rights of others. This respectful regard for others *must be taught* to our children, and it must be taught *both* in our homes and in our schools.

In order for freedom to exist, there must be order, and order bears with it certain responsibilities and obligations. Rules and regulations must be followed, and the consequences for not following them must be established. *There can be freedom only if order is established and observed.*

The crux of the matter is that traditionally kids have not had a voice in the formulation of rules, regulations, codes of conduct, or consequences for violations—the processes by which order is established—and children sense this lack of participation in the processes that establish order.

As a result, we are often confronted with young people's refusal to respect order or to follow the rules, regulations, and codes of conduct that have been imposed upon them. In these cases, kids do not perceive the negative consequences of their actions as the result of poor choices and decisions they have made, but rather as punishment imposed upon them by those who rule over them, primarily their parents and teachers.

Thus, a system of order, *agreed upon by the group*, both at home and in the school setting, must be established. Young people must be given a voice by being included in the establishment of the rules, codes of conduct, consequences for violations, and restrictions by which they are expected to comply. Indeed, they are more likely to abide by the rules if they have had a voice in establishing them.

Children must develop a sense of their own freedom and personal rights before they can be taught to respect the freedom and rights of others, whether it be at home, in the school setting, or in the larger society. Once kids have been given a voice in the establishment of these codes of conduct, rules, and regulations—and consequences for violations—they then can be taught the principles and restrictions necessary for group living and democratic citizenship. This is much more effective than the outdated and resented "forced compliance" still used in most schools and homes throughout the country today.

TEACHING OUR KIDS THE PRINCIPLES OF DEMOCRACY

Democratic beliefs are formed through social experiences, by modeling after significant adults, and practicing the skills involved, yet, again, most schools and homes are clearly not democratic places. John Dewey (1916) advocated that schools should offer students the very qualities that characterize a democratic society—shared interests, freedom in interaction, participation, and social relationships.

According to Malone (2008), democratic civic education should not only instill democratic values and principles in children but also develop critical thinking and problem-solving skills, engage students in debates on a variety of political issues, and provide them with opportunities and experiences in school and community service.

Angell (1991) suggests that free expression, peer interaction in cooperative activities, respect for diverse viewpoints, and student participation in decision making affect future citizenship. She argues that democratic classroom climates are essential to democratic citizenship.

Too often society places the most emphasis on higher education, yet the elementary school has a far greater influence on the development of self-identity in children. Teaching the cultural values of democracy to elementary and middle school children has profound implications in the effort to raise good citizens. It is here where the groundwork is laid for young people's entry into the democratic community of responsible adults. Acting as models of "democratic principles in action," schools should help students understand the nature of citizenship and teach them the knowledge and skills necessary to maintain a democracy (Apple and Beane, 1995).

RAISING GOOD DEMOCRATIC CITIZENS

The bottom line is that democracy must be experienced to be learned, or as Aristotle said, "For the things we have to learn before we can do them, we learn by doing them."

There is more and more emphasis being put on the importance of teaching our young people democratic principles in our public schools. Newspaper columnists, teachers' unions and associations, public organizations, and other civic-minded people are suddenly becoming aware that our young people are growing up ignorant of, and uncommitted to, the great principles upon which our nation was founded (Apple and Beane, 1995).

The simple truth of the matter is that our young people are not committed to democratic principles, political freedom, or the Bill of Rights because they do not experience any of these matters in their everyday life and, in particular, in their schools and homes. In most instances, children do not have rights, they do not participate in making decisions (even when the decisions affect their own lives), and they do not have the freedom of self-determination.

The way to make children committed to our American democratic way of life is to make them full participants in it. If we make our schools and homes models of democracy, give our kids the freedom of choice, and bestow on them the basic rights of citizenship, they will have no trouble understanding what our country is about.

A NEW AGE OF DEMOCRATIC SCHOOLS

There are now various schools around the country that provide children with a democratic education. The Sudbury schools is an example, with 32 K–12 schools in 18 states, as of 2018. Students have complete responsibility for their own education, and students and staff have an equal vote.

Corsini's "Individual Education: A Democratic Model" (2007) is another example. It is an educational model based on democratic principles and Adlerian philosophy that emphasizes the development of student responsibility for their own learning and behavior.

The model is constructed around the implementation of the Four R's: responsibility, respect, resourcefulness, and responsiveness. Responsiveness is the benchmark of a fully functioning human being, according to Alfred Adler (Dreikurs, 1968). It is a feeling for community, social interest, feeling of belonging, and concern for others.

Corsini's school contains three curriculums: *academic* (language arts, math, science, and such), *creative* (areas outside of academics such as cooking, computers, dance, and art), and *social* (problem-solving, social skills, health maintenance, identity development, and so on). A mastery model of achievement is used, and a progress chart replaces report cards and grades. Grade levels are not used.

Discipline is based on natural and logical consequences, and there are only three school rules: (1) do not do anything that could be dangerous or harmful; (2) always be in a supervised place or *en route* from one place to another; and (3) if a teacher signals you to leave the classroom, follow the "Go" signal and leave immediately and in silence. Research suggests increased achievement in the Corsini Democratic School, a decrease in student absenteeism, a decrease in teacher absences, and a decrease in disciplinary problems (Corsini, 2007).

CREATING A DEMOCRATIC CLIMATE IN SCHOOLS AND HOMES

We must turn from the obsolete autocratic dictatorship of demanding submission to a new order based on the democratic principles of freedom and responsibility. Our young people can no longer be forced into compliance—they must be stimulated and encouraged to voluntarily participate in the maintenance of order. They must feel included in the process of making codes of conduct and rules to live by, as well as participate in determining the consequences for failure to comply.

Our youngsters must be taught and allowed to take on responsibility for their own decisions and actions, as well as the subsequent logical and natural consequences, thus giving them a sense of self-worth and empowerment. Once a system is established where dignity, respect, and freedom to make choices is bestowed upon our young people, then the principles of responsibility, obligation, and respect for order can be learned.

Parents, educators, and other significant adults must unite, get on the same page, play on the same team, and *share* the responsibility of our kids' guidance and training. Schools and homes must provide a warm, caring, and respectful environment based on democratic principles where kids can achieve, succeed, flourish, and thrive.

Parents and educators must unite as *democratic leaders* to guide, coach, and stimulate our young people to assume responsibility for themselves. We must guide them in acquiring the skills necessary to make healthy decisions for the direction of their own lives.

It is becoming more and more apparent that without new methods based on democratic principles for dealing with our children—to replace the obsolete, traditional, dictatorial ones—the present confusion of the adult population in dealing with its young will have little chance of being resolved. As a consequence, the incidence of maladjustment, deficiency, and outright rebellion and violence found among many of today's kids will most likely continue to rise.

This handbook for creating a democratic climate to encourage positive behaviors in today's kids is provided to assist educators—teachers, counselors, administrators, and other school personnel—as well as parents, guardians, and caregivers, in creating a caring, respectful, and democratic climate in which children can function more fully as self-directing, self-managing, and self-determining human beings.

Basic communication and counseling tools are provided to not only assist you in helping your children, but also to be beneficial in relating to others in general. Behavior management tips are provided to minimize misbehaviors before they occur, and brief summaries of various classroom discipline models are provided to assist educators and parents in building or rebuilding their own personal systems of discipline.

The future of our kids, and indeed perhaps the future of our nation, is dependent upon making these fundamental changes in our homes and schools compatible to and consistent with the basic, fundamental democratic principles of our larger society.

REFERENCES AND RESOURCES

Angell, A. (1991). Democratic climates in elementary classrooms: A review of theory and research. *Theory and Research in Social Education, 19,* 241–266.

Apple, M., and Beane, J. (Eds.). (1995). *Democratic schools.* Alexandria, VA: Association for Supervision and Curriculum Development.

Blake, S., Brady, T., and Sanchez, S. (2004). Enculturation of democratic principles in the young: A vision of equity education in public schools. *Educational Research Quarterly, 28*(1), 48–59.

Corsini, R. (2007). Corsini's individual education: A democratic model. Groups in educational settings [Special issue]. *Group Dynamics: Theory, Research, and Practice, 11*(4), 247–252.

Dinkmeyer, D., and Dreikurs, R. (1963). *Encouraging children to learn.* New York: Hawthorn Books.

Dreikurs, R. (1968). *Psychology in the classroom* (2nd ed.). New York: Harper & Row.

Malone, H. (2008). Civic education in America's public schools: Developing service- and-politically-oriented youth. *Phi Kappa Phi Forum, 88*(2), 24.

2

Key Concepts in the Philosophical Premises

The Power of Encouragement

It is important to remember that all behavior, both good and bad, makes sense to children, in terms of the way in which THEY view their world.

REBELLION AND VIOLENCE AMONG TODAY'S YOUNG PEOPLE

Vandalism, chaos, turmoil, violence, and even outright rebellion and terrorism are spreading into our public schools and communities at an alarming rate. Parents, teachers, and administrators expect schools to be safe havens of learning. Acts of violence disrupt the learning process and have negative effects on students, the school, and the broader community.

In the United States, there are an estimated 55 million students enrolled in pre-kindergarten through grade 12. An annual report, produced jointly by the Bureau of Justice Statistics and National Center for Education Statistics, presented data on school crime and safety in 2018 from national surveys of students, teachers, principals, and postsecondary institutions.

The following startling facts were reported (CDC, 2019):

- Based on the 2017 National Crime Victimization Survey (NCVS), students ages 12 to 18 experienced 827,000 total victimizations.
- From 2000 to 2017, there were 153 casualties (67 killed and 86 wounded) in active shooter incidents at elementary and secondary schools.

- During the 2015–2016 school year, 47 percent of schools reported one or more crime incidents to police.
- From 2000 to 2017, 10 percent of teachers in city schools were threatened with injury by students, with 6 percent in suburban schools and 5 percent in rural schools.

In addition to school violence, the incidence of juvenile crime in our communities is seriously disturbing. The National Center for Juvenile Justice (2019) reports that, in 2017, courts with juvenile jurisdiction handled an estimated 818,900 delinquency cases. In 1960, approximately 1,100 delinquency cases were processed daily. In 2017, juvenile courts handled roughly 2,200 delinquency cases per day.

No ethnic or racial group, no socioeconomic stratum, and no major geographical area is immune. Many schools across the country have tried the "get-tough" approach for dealing with deviant and defiant behavior. However, the approach focuses on the symptoms, rather than attacking the underlying causes of defiant behavior among children, so getting tough with kids is not the solution.

ALL BEHAVIOR HAS SOCIAL MEANING

If we believe in the philosophy that all children can learn, and if we believe that all behavior is learned, then we must agree that all children can learn positive, socially acceptable, self-managing behavior. We are primarily social beings; thus, behavior has social meaning.

Children are dependent upon their group memberships in the home and school environments for their development. What kids "choose" to do depends largely on how they view themselves and others within these social groups, whether it be within the family, the class group, or their circle of friends.

The methods they choose in order to find a place for themselves within the groups can be destructive or constructive, depending upon the view they have of themselves as members of the groups. Since all behavior at home, in the classroom, and in the community has its specific meaning in the social context, the significance of behavior lies in its social consequences. It is important to remember that *all behavior, both good and bad, makes sense to young people in terms of the way in which* they *view their world* (Dreikurs, 1964).

A SENSE OF BELONGING AND SOCIAL INTEREST

Albert (1996b) asserts that behavior is based on choice and students choose their behavior based on their sense of belonging to the group, so if they perceive themselves to be important, worthwhile, and valued by the group, then they will exhibit positive, socially appropriate behavior.

Teachers are in an influential and powerful position to ensure all kids feel a positive sense of belonging. Glasser (1998) is convinced of the importance of meeting children's five basic needs, one of which is to belong. He describes children's basic needs as (1) survival (food, shelter, and freedom from harm), (2) power (sense of importance, considered by others), (3) fun (having a good time emotionally and intellectually), (4) freedom (exercise of choice, self-direction, and responsibility), and (5) belonging (security, comfort, legitimate member of the group). Glasser (1999) is adamant in his assertion that education that does not meet these basic needs is bound to fail.

Social interest is more than a feeling of belonging—it is a key concept in the understanding of behavior. It is the capacity to "give and take." Social interest is a condition in which students begin to see that it is to their advantage to contribute to the welfare of the group. The child with sufficient social interest accepts responsibility not only for himself but also to and for the group. The well-adjusted child has concern, empathy, and compassion for others; thus, cooperation is one of the most important skills a child will learn.

Social interest becomes restricted in kids who are either spoiled or neglected. Doing too much or too little tends to result in the child's feeling that he does not have to be concerned with "cooperative" relationships, which may result in feelings of inferiority or superiority. As Dreikurs (1964) points out, this maladjustment may ultimately lead to defiant, insolent, even rebellious and violent behaviors. According to Albert (1989), there are four main goals of misbehavior:

1. *Attention-Getting*: When acceptable means are no longer effective, the child will try any method that results in his being noticed. The child would rather be punished than ignored.
2. *Power*: If the adult gets into a power struggle with the child and wins, the child is only more convinced of the value of power and is more determined to win next time.

3. *Revenge:* Revenge is the result of violent antagonism. The child finds his place in the group by making himself disliked.
4. *Inadequacy:* The child "expects" failure. He uses inability or assumed disability to escape participation.

Teachers and parents can influence student behavior, but they cannot directly control it. This is because kids always choose their behavior, even when it is contrary to teacher or parent demands. However, by understanding which goal youngsters hope to achieve through misbehavior, and by applying an intervention strategy for that goal, parents and teachers can exert positive influence on behavior choices that kids make.

The home and the school are support systems that provide children with feedback about themselves. The systems validate children's perceptions of and expectations for others. Children receive support in handling emotions and controlling impulses. Traditionally, we tell children what is expected of them, we make decisions for them, we tell them what to do and when to do it, we watch what they do, and we judge their performance. But does the child feel that he or she is really important within the social group?

The need to be part of the group and to find one's significance through belonging explains many kinds of behavior. Positive, socially acceptable behavior can be measured by the child's ability to cooperate and his willingness to respect the rules of the group. The feelings of belonging to a group and a concern for its common welfare are vital for the social development of the child, which, in turn, is essential for the child's emotional and intellectual development (Dreikurs, 1964).

THE POWER OF ENCOURAGEMENT
The role of both the parent and the educator in this approach is to create a helping relationship in which the child experiences the necessary freedom to explore the areas of his or her life where responsible control is needed. This is accomplished through *encouragement*, one of the most important aspects of any corrective measure.

No child would switch to the socially unacceptable side of life if he were not "discouraged" in his belief that he has a useful place in the group and can succeed with useful means. The extent to which discouragement is rampant in our society can be understood best in the extent to which we see deviant behavior and deficiency in children. Without encouragement, children's growth is stunted, and their potential is inhibited.

Encouragement is so crucial that the effect of any action is actually determined by the extent to which the child is or is not encouraged. To "encourage" means "to give courage to." The opposite of the word *courage* is the word *fear*. We do not seem to have a problem with understanding the emotional connotation given to fear, but I doubt if most people realize that "courage" is just as emotionally powerful.

Encouragement is accomplished by bestowing upon the child a sense of self-worth, dignity, respect, and the rights of self-direction and self-determination, acting consistently upon the belief that he has sufficient capacity to deal constructively with emotional, social, and academic situations, given the proper guidance (Dreikurs, 2009). Learning through encouragement means not only saying, "Good job," but including, "I knew you could do that!" It is sending the message that it is OK to try, and failure is not a crime.

You encourage a child when you provide plenty of opportunities for successful achievement, when you are pleased with a reasonably good attempt at a task, and when you show confidence in the child's ability to become socially and academically competent.

Achievement is the core of the child's role in America's schools. Experiences of success and failure saturate academic life. If a child falls short of his aspirations for academic achievement, and if he experiences few successes in school life, he will have to cope in some way with an inferior self-image and lowered self-esteem. Developing a sense of competence in one's self is crucial to acquiring a positive self-image. *A child who does not know what he is good at will not know what he is good for. He must know what he can do in order to know who he is.*

Encouragement means accepting children as they are—liking them as they are, so they can like themselves. It is showing faith in youngsters and their abilities, so they can have self-respect and faith in themselves. Once children move voluntarily in the right direction as a result of intrinsic, self-motivated choices, the chances are they will continue to do so without outside influence.

What a child decides to do depends largely on his own beliefs, his perceptions of himself in relation to the group, and his methods of finding a place for himself within the social structures of the home, the classroom, the larger school environment, and the neighborhood or community in which he lives.

Through the attitudes of genuine caring, respect, unconditional acceptance, understanding, encouragement, and egalitarian treatment within the group, the child is able to loosen his defenses and rigid perceptions of himself, his home, his school, and his world—and move to higher levels of emotional, social, and intellectual functioning (Dreikurs, 2009).

CREATING NEW CONDITIONS FOR DEMOCRATIC LEARNING

Another major concept of this approach is to create new conditions for learning. The rationale is that, first, all behavior is learned and, second, that appropriate, socially acceptable, self-enhancing behavior is learned more readily in a warm, caring, and democratic environment where kids of all ages have a voice in making decisions that concern their lives.

This approach attempts to facilitate kids in learning the skills necessary to obtain a greater degree of social independence and personal freedom and, at the same time, teaches them to realize their obligations and responsibilities as members of democratic social groups. In other words, a democratic climate is provided conducive to assisting children in moving toward becoming more self-managing individuals, capable of abiding by the rules, codes of conduct, regulations, and restrictions of their various social settings, thus enabling them to deal with problems they face in the future, as well as present.

This approach to guiding children in a democratic environment focuses on their capacity to discover new ways to function more fully as self-directing and self-determining human beings. It is based on the assumption that the desire to move toward emotional growth, social adjustment, and self-management is deeply rooted in the human nature of all children.

In summary, new methods and techniques based on democratic principles to encourage self-direction, respect and compassion for others, respect for order, cooperation, and teamwork is needed to replace the obsolete autocratic traditions of punishment and intimidation.

A key concept of this democracy-based approach is to assist children in achieving an enduring understanding of their own mechanisms of adjustment, thereby enabling them to learn to resolve basic problems on their own and make appropriate choices in life situations.

Some combination of an individualized, humanized, and democratized program, allowing children to develop a sense of worth, a sense of belonging, and a sense of importance, surely holds out the best hope of correcting the present upward trend in the increase of unhappy, underachieving, maladjusted, defiant, rebellious, and even outright violent behavior among even very young children in our society today.

Educators and parents must join forces as democratic leaders to guide, coach, and prepare our young people for entry into the democratic community of responsible adult citizens. Our democratic way of life may depend on it!

REFERENCES AND RESOURCES

Adler, A. (2009). *Social interest: Adler's key to the meaning of life* (Reprint ed.). Oxford: OneWorld.

Albert, L. (1989). *A teacher's guide to cooperative discipline: How to manage your classroom and promote self-esteem*. Circle Pines, MN: American Guidance Service.

Albert, L. (1996b). *Cooperative discipline*. Circle Pines, MN: American Guidance Service.

Centers for Disease Control and Prevention. (2018). School-associated student homicides—United States, 1992–2016. *Morbidity and Mortality Weekly Report, 57*(2), 33–36. Last reviewed October 24, 2019.

Centers for Disease Control and Prevention. (2018). Youth risk behavior surveillance—United States, Surveillance Summaries. Last reviewed August 22, 2018.

Dreikurs, R. (1964). *Children: The challenge*. New York: Hawthorn/Dutton.

Dreikurs, R. (2009). *Child guidance and education: Collected papers of Rudolf Dreikurs*. New York: Alfred Adler Institute.

Glasser, W. (1998b). *The quality school: Managing students without coercion.* New York: HarperCollins.

Glasser, W. (1999). *Choice theory: A new psychology of personal freedom*. New York: HarperCollins.

Glasser, W. (2001). *Every student can succeed*. Chatsworth, CA: William Glasser.

Hockenberry, S., and Puzzanchera, C. (2019). Juvenile court statistics 2017. *OJJD Fact Sheet*. Office of Juvenile Justice and Delinquency, U.S. Department of Justice. Retrieved from http://www.ncjj.org/pdf/jcsreports/jcs2017report.pdf.

3

Some Basic Counseling Tools

You, as educators, parents, and guardians, are in the position to make a truly positive and enduring difference in children's lives.

A word of caution from the beginning—except for licensed school counselors, educators are not permitted to counsel children per se; nor are they allowed to meet with students on an ongoing basis, even to deal with school-related problems, without written parental permission. However, knowledge of some basic communication skills and counseling tools may prove helpful—not only in helping your children with behavior problems and concerns but also in understanding others and yourself more completely. Moreover, the material presented here may be helpful in developing competence in relating to others in general.

You, as educators, parents, and guardians, are in the position to make a truly positive and enduring difference in children's lives. The core communication and counseling concepts presented here are meant for you to use as tools yet maintain your individuality and personal genuineness when relating to others. The goal is that by combining the ideas and strategies presented here with your own knowledge and experience as educators, parents, and other significant adults in kids' lives, you will be better prepared to help your children make positive choices for their lives.

The first goal in developing a helping relationship with children is to provide a warm, caring, respectful, trusting, and safe climate conducive to getting kids involved in self-exploration. As the helper, your attitude assists in creating this climate by being accepting, nonjudgmental, empathetic, and respectful.

The focus of this helping relationship is on the child's responsibility and capacity to discover more appropriate behavior for himself/herself. This is based on the view that the desire to move toward psychological maturity is deeply rooted in the nature of all human beings (Rogers, 1961), including children.

Considered the "father" of person-centered counseling, Carl Rogers often worked with children, and he believed that the young individual has within himself/herself vast resources for self-understanding and for altering his/her self-concept, attitudes, and self-directed behavior. And he believed that these resources can be tapped into if a warm, caring, unconditionally accepting climate is provided.

Helpers use empathetic understanding to communicate an unconditional, positive regard in order to build rapport and create a safe environment in which children can participate in self-exploration (Gibson, Mitchell, & Basile, 1993). Blum (1998) describes being empathetic as showing accurate and sensitive awareness of children's feelings, aspirations, values, beliefs, and perceptions.

Although you may use these communication skills and basic counseling tools with people of any age, imagine that you are using them with your students in school or your children at home. The core communication skills and basic counseling tools in this chapter include the following: active listening, reflecting the content, reflecting feeling, effective inquiry, confronting, goal setting, problem solving, decision making, conflict resolution, and group resolution.

ACTIVE LISTENING

Active listening involves carefully focusing on and following what another person is saying. According to Evans, Hearn, Uhleman, and Ivey (1979, p. 13), "Very few people in our society are effective listeners; most of us find it difficult to focus our attention on others and their comments." This is especially true of adults listening to children. As Dreikurs points out in his book, *Children: The Challenge* (1964), "It is part of our general prejudice against children that we are inclined to assume that we know what they mean without really listening to them" (p. 262).

Active listening demonstrates one's interest in and understanding of what a child is saying and is the foundation of the entire counseling process. The following indicators are *characteristic of a good active listener*:

1. *Maintain appropriate eye contact.* Eye contact is an obvious indication of your interest or lack of interest in what the child is saying. Be aware of frequent breaks in eye contact when listening to them as this indicates a failure to focus on what they are saying. On the other hand, an unwavering stare would most likely make the children feel uncomfortable and less likely to share ideas, thoughts, and feelings.
2. *Maintain a natural but attentive posture.* Assume a relaxed, forward-leaning body position to indicate you are interested. Sitting too straight or too slouched adversely affects the communication process.
3. *Use appropriate facial expressions.* Facial expressions show that you are empathic and understand what the youngster is feeling. For example, if a child is telling you that she feels sad because her best friend just moved away, it would not be appropriate to be smiling. It is important to connect with the child emotionally.
4. *Engage in meaningful gestures.* As the young person is relating a situation to you, you might nod your head, say "uh-huh" or "I see," or reflect back what is being said (*So what you're saying is . . .*) to show you are interested in, focused on, and understanding what is being said.
5. *Be aware of your tone of voice and rate of speech.* A rapid, sharp voice or a bored, tired voice adversely influences the communication process. Maintain a voice that is warm and expressive.

REFLECTING THE CONTENT

Reflecting the content is a skill you acquire to show that you understand what the young person is saying either by *restating* what has been said, *paraphrasing* a single statement in your own words, or *summarizing* a number of statements. One usually begins with, *So, what you're saying is . . .*, and in your own words you restate the essence of what the young person is saying to communicate that you are following and attempting to understand what is being said.

Children often present their ideas in a haphazard way, and by reflecting the content of what they are saying, you can help them organize their thoughts in a concise and accurate manner. In the following example, choose the correct response for reflecting the content:

Student: (Upon the teacher's request, the student stays after school to talk to her.) *I'm not really sure why you wanted to talk to me, unless it's because I haven't been turning in my homework.*

a. Teacher: *I'm sure you know very well why I've called you in to see me.*
b. Teacher: *You think that not doing your homework is causing you problems.*
c. Teacher: *We do have to talk about your failure to do your homework.*

The second response, b, is correct. The essence of the statement is paraphrased without changing the meaning.

REFLECTING FEELING

Reflecting feeling is a skill that requires that you identify the emotions that the young individual is experiencing. Reflection of feelings is a way of letting children know how we recognize and understand their feelings, as well as assisting young individuals in recognizing, understanding, and owning their feelings. This is why the reflecting method usually begins with, "So you feel . . ."

When identifying the emotions of children, it is important to pay attention to not only *what* is being said but also to *how* it is being said. The voice, facial expressions, posture, and mannerisms of young individuals often provide important information about their emotions. In the following example, choose the response that best reflects the student's feelings:

Student: (Describing difficulties getting homework done) *I try, honestly I do, but there's so much noise at home I just can't concentrate on my homework. No matter how hard I try, I can't seem to get it done.*

a. Teacher: *So, you are feeling depressed.*
b. Teacher: *So, you are feeling that working hard doesn't get you anywhere.*
c. Teacher: *So, you are feeling discouraged.*

The last response, c, is the correct reflection of feeling in which you identify the emotion associated with the student's statements and reflect it appropriately.

EFFECTIVE INQUIRY

Effective inquiry requires a knowledge of open inquiry, closed inquiry, and minimal encouragements. Before you can make effective inquiries, you must listen carefully to what is being said. This skill depends on the ability to focus and follow.

Open Inquiry. This method facilitates communication by obtaining information. An open inquiry, also referred to as an open-ended question, requires a more elaborate response than a "yes" or "no" or a simple fact. There are four ways to implement open inquiries:

1. Questions that begin with *what* usually elicit factual information:
   - *What did you do when Sam took the ball away from you?*
2. Questions that begin with *how* encourage the student to give a personal view of the situation:
   - *How did the problem with Sam begin?*
3. Questions that begin with *could, could you,* or *can you* encourage a detailed response:
   - *Could you describe what happened between you and Sam on the playground?*
4. Questions that begin with *why* often help to determine the motive for a behavior but may also make the student defensive. "*Why*" questions have to be worded carefully:
   - *Why did you hit Sam?—Because he took the ball away from me.*
   - NOT: *Why are you always fighting on the playground?*

The second one is more likely to elicit a defensive response such as *Sam started it, not me!*

Closed Inquiry. Also called closed-ended questions, they are used to obtain more precise information and usually elicit a "yes," "no," or simple fact. For example, *Did you tell a teacher on the playground what happened between you and Sam?* or *Who threw the first punch?*

Minimal Encouragements. The repetition of one or two key words in a conversation to encourage the youngster to continue talking is one type of minimal encouragement. Other examples are: *Oh, so, then, go on, hmmm, uh-huh, sure,* or *right.* For example:

> Student: *Sam wouldn't let me play soccer with him.*
>
> Teacher: *Go on.*

CONFRONTING

In daily usage, we often consider confrontation to be hostile or punitive in nature. In counseling, however, confrontation is a high-level skill in which the helper brings attention to discrepancies between verbal and nonverbal behavior. This skill is used only with those individuals with whom you have a good rapport. Confrontation is based on effective listening and careful observation of behavior and should be tentative and nonjudgmental.

When confronting, bring attention to specific discrepancies in actions, in words, and between actions and words. For example: (Tearfully) *I don't want to play soccer with Sam anyway.* Attention is brought to the fact that what is being said does not match the behavior (crying). Another example is: (Laughing) *I wanted to play soccer with Sam, but he wouldn't let me.* Again, what he is saying does not match the observable behavior.

Tentative confrontations often begin with *Could it be . . .* or *You tend to suggest . . .*: *I am noticing that you are laughing as you tell me about Sam not letting you play soccer with him. Could it be that you are not really feeling happy about this situation?*

Beware of the young individual's feelings before and after the confrontation. Reflections of feelings may be necessary to encourage the youngster to face the discrepancies. Effective confrontations often lead to a clearer understanding of the problem for both parties and to constructive change in behavior.

GOAL SETTING

Goal setting is useful when assisting an individual to achieve a desired target. It is important that the individual see the goal as worthwhile and attainable, with a specific time frame to achieve it. It needs to be realistic and achievable, given past experiences, as well as independent of another person's actions. The goal should be positive for all concerned and considerate of others. The goal-setting process has the following steps:

1. State the Goal
   - Identify and write a goal that meets the above criteria. Again, make sure it is something the individual really wants to achieve.
   - *What do you want to happen?*
2. Identify the Roadblocks
   - Identify possible barriers to achieving the goal.
   - Specify ways to overcome the barriers.
3. Make the Plan of Action
   - List the steps required to achieve the goal.
   - *What are the steps you will need to take in order to reach your goal?*
4. Evaluation
   - Note the progress of achievement of each step.
   - *How well did your plan work?*
   - *Did you reach your goal?*
   - *What changes might you make for next time?*
5. Celebrate the Success!
   - *Good job in achieving your goal!*
   - *I knew you could do it!*

An example of an academic goal might be to improve a math grade, and it might look like this:

Goal: To earn a higher grade in math.
Roadblocks:

1. Too noisy at home to concentrate on homework
   - Ask family to give you some quiet time to work.
   - Go to a neighbor's house where it is quieter to do homework.

2. No one to help when I have questions.
   - Find a classmate to be a peer tutor.
   - Find someone, like a neighbor or relative, who would be willing to help you.

Steps to Achieve the Goal: (Keep a daily checklist of steps)

1. Complete all daily assignments.
2. Study for tests and quizzes.
3. Participate in class.
4. Pay attention to the teacher.
5. Ask for help when unsure.
6. Respond positively to constructive criticism.
7. Cooperate in group situations.
8. Work well alone.

Evaluation:
   - *After following the above steps, was there an improvement in your math grade?*
   - *What additional changes could you make for the next grading period?*

PROBLEM-SOLVING SKILLS

Problem-solving is one of the most important skills kids can learn. C. M. Charles (2013) discusses Coloroso's views on the importance of kids learning to distinguish between *reality* and *problem*, "with reality being an accurate appraisal of what has occurred in a situation and problem being the discomfort being caused by the reality" (p. 223). Coloroso points out that in learning to solve problems, we accept the realities, then we solve the problems that come from them.

When students understand this distinction, they realize there is no problem so great it cannot be solved. The next step is to teach students a plan of attack for solving their problems. Here is a basic problem-solving model:

1. Identify and define the problem specifically until all individuals involved understand the problem.

2. Brainstorm all possible solutions to the problem.
3. Delete the options that are unsatisfactory, such as those that are unkind, unfair, dishonest, or hurtful.
4. Evaluate and examine the possible consequences of the remaining options.
5. Select one best option.
6. Make a plan for the selected option and agree to try it.
7. Evaluate and revise the plan as necessary.

DECISION-MAKING SKILLS

Teaching kids to make decisions for themselves has many benefits in both the school and home settings. It makes them more self-reliant and self-directing and encourages them to think things through. The best way to teach children decision-making skills is to bring them to situations that call for decisions, allow them to make decisions while the educator or parent provides guidance without judgment, and let them experience the results, the natural consequences, of their decisions. Mistakes and poor choices are now the students' responsibility. If they experience discomfort, they have the power to make better decisions in the future.

When children are given ownership of problems and situations, they know it is up to them to make matters better. They have no one else to blame. What they need is the opportunity to correct the situation they have created. You might want to say something like, *You have a problem. What is your plan?*

Teachers and parents are there to offer advice, support, and even options—but not solutions. This allows students to take responsibility for their mistakes, rather than blaming them on someone or something else. One might follow these steps when making decisions:

1. Identify the goal of the decision to be made.
2. Investigate and gather information about the situation.
3. List the possible choices for the decision.
4. Specify the probable consequences of each choice.
5. Evaluate each choice by its consequences:
   - *Will it help meet the identified goal of the decision?*
   - *What are the advantages of that choice? Disadvantages?*
   - *What are the risks?*

- *How will it affect others?*
- *How will I feel about this choice?*

6. Rank the choices by priority.
7. Make a decision by selecting one choice.
8. Make a plan to put the decision in effect.
9. Follow through with the plan.
10. Evaluate the consequences of the decision.

CONFLICT RESOLUTION

Having rules for "fighting fair" helps kids switch from fighting and getting nowhere to actually resolving their conflicts. Once mastered, these are skills that can be used in a variety of situations and will serve them well throughout life. It takes time to learn new behaviors, so it is important to help kids keep trying.

Fighting fair is an art, and it needs to be taught both at home and in school. Our kids are learning how to treat each other through watching television shows, movies, and video games, as well as watching how significant adults, especially parents and teachers, relate to each other and *to them*. As their role models, when you get upset with your kids, what kind of an example are you setting for when they get upset with others? Here are some simple, but not necessarily easy, rules for fighting fair—not only for kids but also for adults:

1. Don't call names or put others down.
2. If you are upset, walk away from the situation to cool off.
3. Timing is important. If emotions are high, schedule the "fight" for a time agreeable to both parties. Pick a location that is private and neutral.
4. Focus on the problem, not on the person.
5. Deal with one issue at a time.
6. Stay focused on the present; it's not fair to bring up past grievances.
7. State the conflict clearly and stay focused on the problem.
8. Take turns speaking and listening. Be willing to listen to what the other person has to say without interrupting.
9. Brainstorm possible solutions to the problem.
10. Agree on one solution that will work for all parties. Be willing to compromise.

11. Try out the solution. If it doesn't work, schedule another time to meet and choose another solution to try.
12. Be willing to forgive. Nobody is perfect, and we all make mistakes.

The following phrases are important to keep in mind when fighting fair:

- *How can we work this conflict out together?*
- *This is what I would like to see happen.*
- *This is what I am willing to do.*
- *What would you like to see happen?*
- *What would you be willing to do?*

When conflicts occur in the school setting, which they inevitably will, educators are expected to diffuse the situation. The two common types of conflict resolution are the *Win-Lose* method and the *No-Lose* method (also known as the *Win-Win* method).

The Win-Lose Method. In this method, the ego is on the line, and when the conflict is resolved, one person emerges as "winner" and the other as "loser." Imagine the following scenario: Betty keeps talking across the aisle to Susan. Susan gets frustrated by the interruptions and says to the teacher, *Betty keeps talking to me and I can't get my work done.* The teacher tells Betty to move to another desk so she can't bother Susan anymore. Betty moves but is seething with resentment. Susan emerges the "winner" and Betty is the "loser," or so it would seem. In reality, both may have lost, because their friendship may have been jeopardized.

The No-Lose Method. Instead of using the win-lose approach, Gordon advocates the no-lose method in resolving conflicts. This approach allows both parties to find a mutually acceptable solution to their conflict. In the above scenario, the teacher might have gone over to Betty and said, *Could you please explain what is happening here?* Betty answers, *I don't know how to do this assignment, and I was just asking Susan for help.* The teacher replies, *Can you think of another way you could have asked for help without disrupting Susan?* Betty replies, *I could have raised my hand and asked you to help me.* The teacher assures her that would have been a much better choice, and the conflict is resolved. Both sides emerge as winners, so it was a *no-lose*, or *win-win* resolution.

Resolution of more serious conflicts or repeated violations of the class code of conduct should be done in a conference. The purpose of the conference is not to put the blame on the student but, rather, to assist him in working out ways for him to behave more responsibly. Albert, in her work *Comparative Discipline* (1989), outlines her "Six-D Conflict Resolution Plan." It is a useful tool for resolving problems in dispute, whether it takes place between students in the classroom or siblings at home. The plan is composed of the following six steps:

1. *Define* the problem objectively. Do not blame or use emotional words.
2. *Declare* the need. Tell what makes the situation a problem.
3. *Describe* the feelings experienced by both parties.
4. *Discuss* possible solutions. Consider the pros and cons of each option.
5. *Decide* on a plan. Choose the solution that has the most support from both parties. Be specific about when the plan will begin.
6. *Determine* the effectiveness of the plan. After the plan has been in effect for a time, arrange a follow-up meeting to evaluate its effectiveness.

In some instances, the educator or parent may help *an individual child* resolve his conflict, dispute, or problem by working with him on a one-on-one basis. Other instances require helping *two individuals* resolve a dispute between them. The following is a practical step-by-step description of an educator helping an *individual* resolve a conflict or problem using "I Messages":

1. The student comes to you for help with a conflict. You respond, *Do you want to tell me about your conflict (problem)?* Whenever possible phrase your questions for choices. *Do you want . . .* creates a different feeling than *Tell me about . . .*(a command form of the verb) or *What is your conflict?* (which is a question demanding an answer). When you ask, *Do you want . . .*, the individual has the choice to tell you or not. Also, when he answers, "Yes," it instills a sense of commitment on his part.
2. *Restate and reflect content and feelings.* Stop frequently to restate in your own words what the individual is saying and feeling. Sometimes a person says one thing and means another, or his nonverbal communication, such as facial expressions, gestures, and so on, are not reflective of what he is

really feeling. By restating and reflecting, you help clarify the facts, as well as the feelings, for both of you.

Let's look at your conflict again using the "I Message" format. How would you fill in these blanks?

- I feel (felt) _____ when _____ because _____ and I need/want _____.

He may answer something like:

- I feel *very sad* when *Danny doesn't let me play soccer with him at recess* because *it makes me feel like he doesn't want to be my friend*, and I want *you to talk to him about letting me play soccer with him.*

Now you know what the conflict is, how the student is feeling, and what he needs or wants done to resolve the conflict. If it is a conflict involving another person, such as the one described here, you might give him a blank "I Message" form and suggest he take it home and fill it out as if he were directly talking to, or confronting, the other person. It might read something like this:

- Hey, Danny, could I talk to you for a second? I feel *very sad* when *you don't let me play soccer with you at recess* because *it makes me feel like you don't want to be my friend*, and I want *you to let me play on your team with you.* Would you be willing to *let me play soccer with you guys?*

In other words, encourage him to confront Danny with his conflict. Ask him if he would be willing to give it a try.

3. *Brainstorm possible solutions.* In the case above, the student might list "Confront Danny" as one of the options. Other solutions might be "Find another group of kids and make my own soccer team," or "Try to work out the conflict by meeting with Danny in a counseling session with the counselor." Have the student think of all the possible solutions he might try.
4. *Choose one option to try and do it.*
5. *Evaluate the choice.* Did it resolve the conflict? If not, go back to step 4 and choose another option.

If the person is unwilling or unable to resolve the conflict on his own, then the educator or parent may need to assist him. The following is a step-by-step description of conflict resolution strategies for resolving a dispute *between two individuals*:

1. Say: *It has been brought to my attention that there might be a conflict between the two of you.* (Notice that no names are mentioned. This starts the two individuals out on more of an even keel, rather than saying, *Judy here told me she has a problem with you.*)
2. Then ask the first person (the one who is more upset), *Would you like help resolving this conflict?* Then ask the second person, *Would you be willing to help resolve this conflict?* Both parties have to agree before the resolution process can proceed.

   Inform them: *There are five ground rules you both need to agree to follow:*
   - No put-downs or name calling.
   - Just state the facts as honestly as you can.
   - No interrupting when someone is talking.
   - Agree to work on resolving the conflict.
   - Remain calm.

Again, turn toward the one who is more upset and say, *Do you agree to these ground rules?* Then ask the other one.

   Ask the first person to tell his/her side of the story, using the "I Message" format. Have the second person *restate and reflect* the message. Then reverse the roles and allow the second person to tell his side:
   - First person fills in the blanks: I felt _____ when (you) _____ because _____.
   - Second person restates and reflects what the problem is for the other person: So you felt _____ when (I) _____ because _____?
   - After the second person restates the problem, he/she may ask questions to understand the situation better.

3. Ask: *What are some possible solutions to this problem?* Both individuals brainstorm possible solutions. (The educator or parent may also suggest solutions while writing down the suggestions.) If one of the individuals is

not participating, remind him/her about ground rule 4, *agreeing to work on resolving the conflict.*
4. Both individuals agree on a resolution. As you write down their suggestions, be looking for one you think they could both agree to. You may need to make suggestions. A good resolution is fair to both parties and has each person doing something to help solve the problem.

Congratulate both individuals for resolving their problem. For example, the educator or parent might say something like, *I really like the way you both worked to resolve this conflict. I'm impressed with your communication skills,* or *I had a feeling you two would find a solution to your problem.* When working with younger children, you might also ask them to shake hands.

GROUP RESOLUTION STRATEGIES
Classrooms are microcosms of the larger society and, as such, reflect its cultural and ethnic diversity. Culture provides individuals with certain beliefs, attitudes, and expectations in social settings; thus, conflicts are an inevitable aspect of school social groups.

The fact that conflicts exist is not necessarily a bad thing, however. As long as they are resolved effectively, they can promote group and personal growth by (1) increasing understanding of the conflict situation, (2) enhancing awareness of the things that are important to individuals, (3) developing stronger mutual respect, and (4) building confidence in the group's ability to work together. Group resolution should respect individual differences and, at the same time, emphasize the ways in which group members are more alike than different.

Types of Group Conflicts
Conflicts occur in all social settings, and because of the wide range of diversity among students, the absence of conflict usually signals the absence of meaningful interaction. Conflict by itself is neither good nor bad. However, the manner in which conflict is handled determines whether it is constructive or destructive. There are two types of conflicts: *cognitive* (aimed at issues, ideas, principles, or processes) and *affective* (aimed at people, emotions, or values). According to Capozzoli (1995), cognitive conflicts are constructive,

whereas affective conflicts are destructive. He describes the outcomes of constructive and destructive conflicts:

Constructive conflicts exist in these situations:

- People change and grow personally from the conflict.
- The conflict results in a solution to a problem.
- It increases involvement of everyone affected by the conflict.
- It builds cohesiveness among the members of the group

Destructive conflicts exist in these situations:

- No decision is reached, and the problem still exists.
- It diverts attention away from activities of more value.
- It destroys the morale of the group.
- It polarizes or divides the group.

Group Code of Conduct for Resolving Conflicts

It is essential to establish a Code of Conduct, generated by the group members, for resolving group conflicts. The teacher-generated code might include the following steps:

1. Remain calm.
2. Be respectful.
3. Be an active listener.
4. Be open to others' opinions.
5. Attack the problem, not the person.

Have students identify appropriate and inappropriate behaviors for each of the operating principles. It is important to clarify each of the behaviors listed so that every student knows exactly what each suggestion means. This is accomplished through explanations, modeling, and role playing.

A Process of Group Resolution

Students need guidelines to give them structure as they learn about and become involved in the process of resolving group conflicts. The following five-step approach to group resolution is effective:

Step 1: Set the Scene

Allow those students involved in the conflict to state their positions. As an example, there is a school art show being planned, and the class has voted unanimously to participate in it. The teacher has asked the class if they would prefer working on the art projects in cooperative learning groups or individually. A majority of the students vote to work in groups, but a few of the students are adamant about wanting to work on their projects individually. These students are given the opportunity to voice their objections for not going along with the majority. As the students give their viewpoints, the teacher or the class student leader restates, paraphrases, and summarizes the opinions.

Step 2: Gather Information

In this step, you are trying to get to the underlying needs and concerns of the students involved in the conflict. Have the few students elaborate on what their reasons are for wanting to work independently on their art projects. Encourage them to express themselves using "I Messages." Emphasize listening with empathy to their point of view. Perhaps it is revealed that the few students who object to working in groups on this project are quite artistically talented and want the opportunity to show what they can do individually on their art projects. Students representing the sentiment of the majority might express that they do not feel competent doing art projects and working with a group allows them to feel more self-confident and secure.

Step 3: Agree to the Problem

This sounds like an obvious step; however, often different needs, interests, and goals can cause students to perceive problems differently. Every group member must agree to what the problem is in order to find a mutually acceptable solution. It is agreed that the problem is this: Although a majority of the class wants to work on their art projects in small groups, there are four students who have a strong desire to work individually on their projects.

Step 4: Brainstorm Possible Solutions

To ensure that all group members feel satisfied with the resolution, everyone must have a fair voice in generating the solutions. Be open to all ideas.

Step 5: Negotiate a Solution

By this stage, both sides have a better understanding of the positions of the other, and a mutually satisfactory solution may be clear to all. In the example provided, one option might be that the students who prefer group projects may sign up to work in small groups, and the students who want to work independently may sign up for individual projects. Another option might be to assign those students who are artistically talented to the same group, have them make their projects independently, and then combine them in a display. The problem is resolved satisfactorily for all parties involved.

Consensus Decision Making

Some class decisions may require a unanimous agreement, others may require a majority vote, and others may be resolved by the group resolution process described earlier. But there are times when *consensus decision making* is more appropriate. Consensus decision making is a group decision-making process that seeks not only the agreement of most of the students but also the resolution of any objections. It is a process of coming to a general agreement, and it attempts to help everyone get what they need. In this process, students should strive to reach the best possible solution for the group and all of its members. There are various models for consensus decision making, but here are the basic steps:

As a Group:

1. Discuss the decision to be made.
2. Generate a decision proposal.
3. Test for consensus.
4. Identify unsatisfied concerns.
5. Modify the decision proposal to generate as much agreement as possible.
6. Retest for consensus.

Once the group has formulated the decision proposal, test for consensus by having the group members raise the number of fingers that correspond with how they feel about the proposal, using the following key: (1) very satisfied, (2) somewhat satisfied, (3) neutral, (4) somewhat dissatisfied, and (5) very dissatisfied. Allow those students showing four or five fingers to express their concerns.

Modify the proposal to accommodate their concerns and retest for consensus. After a concerted effort has been made at generating full agreement, the group must determine if the existing level of agreement is sufficient to finalize the decision. There may be occasions when the group is unable to reach a consensus on a decision, but generally speaking, a consensus can be reached.

REFERENCES AND RESOURCES

Albert, L. (1989). *A teacher's guide to cooperative discipline: How to manage your classroom and promote self-esteem.* Circle Pines, MN: American Guidance Service.

Blum, D. (1998). *The school counselor's book of lists.* San Francisco, CA: Jossey-Bass.

Brockman, E. (1996). Removing the paradox of conflict from group dynamics. *Academy of Management Executive, 10*(2), 61–62.

Capozzoli, T. (1995). Resolving conflict within teams. *Journal for Quality and Participation, 8*(7), 28–30.

Charles, C. M. (2013). *Building classroom discipline* (11th ed.). New York: Pearson.

Coloroso, B. (1994). *Kids are worth it! Giving your child the gift of inner discipline.* New York: William Morrow.

Deutch, M., and Coleman, P. (Eds.). (2000). *The handbook of conflict resolution: Theory and practice.* San Francisco, CA: Jossey-Bass.

Evans, D., Hearn, M., Uhlemann, M., and Ivey, A. (1979). *Essential interviewing: A programmed approach to effective communication.* Monterey, CA: Brooks/Cole.

Gibson, R., Mitchell, M., and Basile, S. (1993). *Counseling in the elementary classroom: A comprehensive approach.* Boston: Allyn & Bacon.

Hartnett, T. (2011). *Consensus-oriented decision making.* Gabriola Island, BC: New Society Publishers.

Rogers, C. (1961). *On becoming a person.* Boston: Houghton Mifflin.

4

Behavior Management Tips to Minimize Misbehavior

Discipline problems gradually become insignificant when you have a classroom environment where there is a climate of acceptance, respect, dignity and encouragement.

—C. M. Charles, world-renowned expert on classroom discipline

Classroom management is defined as the strategies and methods a teacher uses to maintain a classroom environment that is conducive to student success and learning. Students need to feel they are in an environment that allows them to voice their opinions concerning decisions that affect their lives. From their perspective, classroom management should involve clear communication of behavioral and academic expectations, as well as a cooperative learning environment (Allen, 1986).

Classroom management involves creating a positive classroom community with mutual respect and caring between teacher and student, as well as among students themselves. If teachers express unconditional warmth, acceptance, respect, and support toward students, students will learn to treat each other according to their example. Please note that many of the principles discussed in this chapter are conducive for adaptation to the home setting as well.

Fair rules, better termed a *Code of Conduct*, with consequences for violations of the code, are established by the classroom community with the teacher as their democratic leader. Students should be given frequent and consistent feedback about their behavior.

We all take pleasure in being encouraged, praised, complimented, and rewarded for a job well done, and students are no exception. It is important, however, to provide praise and rewards for *exhibiting specific positive behaviors*, such as persistence, self-discipline, or hard work, rather than as a means of controlling behavior. Teachers must emphasize the value of the behavior being rewarded, as well as explain to students the specific skills they demonstrated to *earn* the reward.

In accordance with many classroom management experts, teachers should also encourage student collaboration in selecting the rewards and defining appropriate behaviors that will *earn* rewards (Bear, Cavalier, & Manning, 2005): *earn* is the key word here. Other experts emphasize the importance of educating kids about the value of internal motivation; the intention is to prompt and develop within children a desire, first, to become responsible and self-disciplined and, second, to put forth effort to learn (Marshall, 2001).

Discipline problems gradually become insignificant when you have a classroom environment where there is a climate of acceptance, respect, dignity, and encouragement. Students need to develop skills in self-control, self-discipline, cooperation, and good decision making. They need to perceive themselves as capable, valued, and in control of their own lives. This type of learning environment is more easily created when you implement the following classroom management strategies:

I. A *Code of Conduct with Consequences for Violations*—generated and agreed upon by the class group.
II. *Class Meetings*—conducted by the class group where such skills as conflict resolution, group resolution, and problem solving can be learned and practiced.
III. *A Peer Mediation Program*—where students mediate disputes between other students.

I. A CODE OF CONDUCT WITH CONSEQUENCES FOR VIOLATIONS
Discussion

For many people, the term *rules* has the implication of being a teacher-imposed policy that kids had better follow or suffer the dire consequences of punishment. For this reason, teachers are strongly advised to work together with their students to establish a *Code of Conduct*. A Code of Conduct specifies how everyone is supposed to behave and interact, including the teacher.

In accordance with the Code of Conduct, every person is held accountable for his or her own behavior at all times. Albert (1996b) would have this classroom Code of Conduct replace the classroom rules that teachers usually use. As she points out, rules cause difficulty because students often interpret the word *rules* as what teachers use to control them. Besides, a Code of Conduct covers a wider variety of behavior, whereas classroom rules are limited in scope.

For the following summary of Albert's development, implementation, and reinforcement of the Code of Conduct concept, a primary resource, *Building Classroom Discipline* (2013), is used with permission from the author, C. M. Charles. Dr. Charles's book is highly recommended for those who seek a more in-depth study of the various models of classroom discipline.

Developing a Code of Conduct

The following is a guide to follow when developing the Code of Conduct:

1. *Envision the ideal.* Spend time thinking about how you would like your classroom to be, if everything were like you wanted. How would students act toward each other? This vision will help you to identify goals for classroom behavior.
2. *Ask students for their vision of how they would like their class group to be.* It is essential to involve students at all levels of this process. Students usually want the same conditions that teachers want, so it will be easy to merge the two visions.
3. *Ask for parents' input.* It is strongly advised involving parents by sending them a letter summarizing the ideas students have expressed and asking for comments and suggestions. This increases parental support for the Code of Conduct.
4. The following is an example of a *teacher-generated code of conduct* from which to build the Class Code of Conduct:
    - I am respectful.
    - I am responsible.

- I am safe.
- I am prepared.

Because "Excellence in Education" is our motto:

- I will do nothing to prevent the teacher from teaching or prevent anyone, myself included, from participating in educational activities.
- I will cooperate with all members of the school community.
- I will treat everyone with respect and courtesy.

Teaching the Code

The Code of Conduct is taught to students by involving them in interpreting the above principles by following these steps:

1. *Identify appropriate and inappropriate behaviors.* First ask students to identify specific behaviors that are appropriate for each operating principle. For example, in discussing what one does when you "treat everyone with respect and courtesy," students might suggest the following *appropriate* behaviors:

   - Listening when others are speaking.
   - Using a pleasant tone of voice.
   - Using proper language.
   - Responding politely to requests from teachers and classmates.

   These are behaviors that students might list as *inappropriate*:

   - Putting others down.
   - Pushing and shoving.
   - Making obscene gestures.
   - Making fun of others.

   It does not matter if these lists get long. Their purpose is to help students develop the understanding necessary for evaluating their own behavioral choices and for accepting responsibility for their own actions.

2. *Clarify appropriate and inappropriate behaviors.* It is not enough just to list student suggestions. They must be clarified so that every student knows exactly what each suggestion means. This is accomplished through explanations, modeling, and role playing.

3. *Involve parents.* Students might write a letter to their parents to explain the Code of Conduct by listing the appropriate and inappropriate behaviors they have identified. The teacher can add a note asking parents to save the letter for discussions with their children.

Enforcing the Code

When enforcing the Code of Conduct, teachers are advised to do the following when misbehavior occurs:

1. *Check for understanding.* Ask questions to make sure students understand that their behavior is inappropriate as it relates to the Code. Here are some examples:
   - What behavior are you choosing at the moment?
   - Is the behavior you are choosing at the moment appropriate to our Code of Conduct?
   - Is this behavior on our appropriate list or inappropriate list of behaviors?
   - Can you help me understand why you are violating our Code of Conduct at the moment?
   - Given our Code of Conduct, what should I say to you right now?
2. *Problem solve when disagreements occur.* Students may sometimes disagree with the teacher as to whether their behavior is appropriate or inappropriate. These disagreements may be resolved in one of three ways:
   - With a private student-teacher conference.
   - In a class meeting dealing with the behavior.
   - By any mediation or conflict-resolution process.
3. *Post the Code of Conduct.* It is a good idea to post the Code of Conduct in the classroom. When prominently displayed, the teacher can do the following things:
   - Walk to the display, point to the principle being violated, and make eye contact with the offending student.
   - Write the number of the principle being violated on a little slip of paper and place it on the offending student's desk.
   - Point to the operating principle being violated and say, Tell me in your own words *what this principle means* (and call on the offending student).

Reinforcement of the Code

It is important to reinforce the Code of Conduct. Frequent repetition and review are needed to help students become proficient in monitoring their behavior. Consider the following suggestions:

1. *Review the Code of Conduct* daily or weekly, depending on the need for review.
2. *Model self-correction.* When the teacher makes a mistake, such as yelling at the students, the violation should be admitted, with an explanation of how it will be done correctly the next time.
3. *Encourage student self-evaluation.* Ask students to make lists of their own behavior that show how they are complying with or violating the Code of Conduct.

Implementing the Consequences

In regard to implementing the consequences when students seriously or repeatedly violate the classroom Code of Conduct, Albert recommends her "4 R's" for implementing them. They should be related, reasonable, respectful, and reliably enforced. There are four categories of consequences for teachers to discuss with their students:

1. *Loss or delay of privileges*, such as loss or delay of a favorite activity.
2. *Loss of freedom of interaction*, such as talking with other students.
3. *Restitution*, such as return, repair, or replacement of objects; doing school service; or helping other students one has offended.
4. *Reteaching appropriate behavior*, such as practicing correct behavior and writing about how one should behave in a given situation.

This plan is designed to help students achieve their ultimate goal of *belonging to the group*. When they sense belonging, and when they find success, students show relatively little misbehavior. Students will misbehave even in the best of settings, but it is strongly suggested that teachers use procedures that emphasize teaching appropriate behavior rather than punishing improper behavior. The Code of Conduct concept may be adapted by parents to use in the home setting as well, involving their children at every level in the formulation of their Family Code of Conduct.

II. CLASS MEETINGS

Discussion

Class meetings help promote a warm, caring, respectful, and supportive learning environment. They encourage a climate where students feel comfortable to learn and achieve, feel safe to share their ideas, and feel free to ask questions and take risks.

Kohn (2001) advocates transforming classrooms into *learning communities* where students feel cared about and are encouraged to care about each other. Teachers establish classrooms conducive to good relationships through the practices of *positivity, choice,* and *reflection* (Kohn, 2005). *Positivity* is an emotion of optimism where the focus is on the benefits and advantages of things, rather than on the negative aspects. *Choice* empowers kids by giving them options to consider. *Reflection* is the process where kids look at their own behavior and determine its effectiveness. Reflection is necessary for positive changes in behavior to occur.

The Rationale

In class meetings, students learn to work cooperatively, to encourage and support each other, to assume responsibility for their own behavior and learning, and to be good decision makers and creative problem solvers. Creating such a climate of mutual respect and trust is necessary in order for each group member to develop the confidence necessary to make statements, voice opinions, and generally contribute to the group processes in a safe and nonthreatening environment. The *rationale* for implementing the Class Meeting concept includes:

1. Students develop a greater sense of responsibility when given a chance to make meaningful contributions to the social group of which they are a member.
2. When students believe they are valued for their contributions to the classroom environment, they feel a sense of belonging and are more motivated to learn.
3. Students who are involved in solving problems and making decisions concerning class issues are more likely to abide by the solutions.

Experts Who Support the Class Meeting Concept

There is an increasing number of experts and authorities in classroom discipline who support the Class Meeting concept. Dreikurs and Cassel's basic idea (1972) is that any "problem child" is a problem for the whole class, and the solution to the problem grows most naturally out of the helpful involvement of all class members. The teacher serves as the group leader and confronts any misbehaving student with his mistaken goal (attention, power, revenge, or inadequacy). Group discussions in the classroom are essential in this democratic setting.

Nelsen, Lott, and Glenn (1997) contend that students need to perceive themselves as capable, significant, and in control of their own lives, and these perceptions grow best in classes that hold regular class meetings. The skills of self-control, adaptability, cooperation, and judgment are best developed in the class meeting setting. Within this model of class meetings, students decide most of the topics, the total class is involved, a specified format is followed, and valuable life skills are learned.

Glasser (1999) strongly believes that misbehavior is simply a bad behavior choice (Choice Theory) and that class meetings would provide an open forum for the entire class to deal with individual and group problems. Having the problem confronted by the entire class makes students aware of their behaviors and promotes responsibility for consequences.

Types of Class Meetings

There are three main types of class meetings: open-ended, educational, and problem solving (Wolfgang, 2001):

1. An *open-ended meeting* addresses imaginary problems that the teacher can pose or that students can create with their own fantasies. Kids practice skills through role playing to gain experience in dealing with the hypothetical problems.
2. The *educational meeting* allows the teacher to address a curriculum topic to assess where the students are on the subject and where they need to be taken.
3. The *problem-solving meeting* focuses on actual problems the class is having, such as stolen items, settling down before a lesson, a specific student who is causing problems, or any other problems the class must solve.

Benefits of Class Meetings

Here are some of the beneficial aspects of class meetings:

- Teachers develop a closer relationship with their students.
- Class meetings give ownership of the class to the students.
- Class meetings provide a setting to gain understanding of how other people feel and think, which are necessary aspects of getting along. This promotes the development of such character qualities as compassion, empathy, respect for others' points of view, and acceptance of those who are culturally or otherwise different from themselves.
- Class meetings provide a venue for the development of essential social skills as students learn to listen attentively to gain real understanding, as well as to listen to each other as they learn respectful and accepting ways of relating. Students learn the value of cooperation, working on a team, and negotiating solutions to problems.
- Students develop a sense of cause and effect and learn that their actions have consequences—positive or negative—to themselves or to other people.
- Students learn values that are fundamental to our democratic system, such as fairness, tolerance, respect, honesty, and loyalty. They learn civil and peaceful ways to deal with different points of view and that there is more than one way to deal with difficult challenges.
- Class meetings provide opportunities for insightful, creative, and critical-thinking processes.
- Class meetings create a sense of community by promoting class cohesiveness. They provide a venue where students talk about subjects and concerns that affect their lives in important ways.

Implementing Class Meetings

Implementing class meetings is not a difficult task if teachers prepare students for meetings in two or three lessons during the first few weeks of school. Teachers will need to provide a "Discussion Box," which can be a decorated shoe box, in the classroom, where students can submit topics for class meeting discussions.

The lessons should involve circle formation and the teaching and modeling of encouragement and creative problem solving. After several meetings with the teacher leading and modeling the process, students become meeting leaders. There are several *key components* that make class meetings effective and successful:

1. Meetings are held every week at a set time, such as every Friday afternoon in the last hour of the day, or every Monday in the first hour or before lunch.
2. Desks are moved to the perimeter of the classroom or to one side, and students sit on chairs in a circle. Desks may also be moved into a "U" formation.
3. A set format for the *Agenda* is followed.
   - Make compliments and show appreciations. A "Random Acts of Kindness" box can be kept in the room, where students can submit reports about acts of kindness they have observed. These may be read during the class meeting.
   - Follow up on prior solutions applied to problems.
   - Go through agenda items on the list (from the "Discussion Box").
   - Share feelings about them.
   - Discuss the issue at hand.
   - Ask for problem-solving help.
   - Practice a specific skill, such as active listening, role playing, or brainstorming.
   - Make future plans for a fun activity, such as a field trip, a "Fun Friday," or a special project.
4. Model respectful and encouraging behaviors.
5. Have faith in the creative problem-solving process.
6. Trust the ability of your students to lead meetings, participate in discussions, and make decisions that will affect their lives at school.

The *role of the teacher* during class meetings includes the following actions:

- Acting as a consultant and coach, providing guidance only when necessary.
- Performing the role of class meeting secretary, with assistance from a student assistant secretary, to take notes during the meetings.
- Participating as a group member, giving assistance only when necessary, keeping the tone positive and helpful, and keeping the class meeting on task and moving forward when necessary.

The *role of the student leader* (who might also be called the class president, elected by the class) during class meetings includes the following actions:

- Opening and closing the meeting.
- Keeping the group on task and on topic.
- Following the order of the agenda.
- Following the steps for solving problems.
- Making eye contact with the person speaking.
- Letting students know when they are out of order.
- Asking questions or restating problems to clarify issues.
- Summarizing ideas.

Creating a Democratic Community

Creating a democratic community in the classroom and fostering a safe, respectful environment empowers kids to make choices and grow into confident, self-directed, successful students. With class meetings, discipline becomes a minor issue. Problems are discussed, and students themselves determine the consequences for misbehavior.

When students choose solutions to problems, they have a stake in seeing that the consequences are followed. Problems in the classroom are no longer just the teacher's to solve; they become the class's problems. Students are highly accountable for their actions when their peers are taking note of their behavior and discussing inappropriate behavior in class meetings.

Practice with the process each week enables students to become excellent problem solvers, coming up with fair and effective methods of helping fellow classmates improve and change behaviors that interfere with others' or with their own learning.

III. A PEER MEDIATION PROGRAM

Discussion

Peer mediation is both a program and a process where students, working in pairs, facilitate resolving disputes between two fellow students or small groups. It is a negotiation-based approach that teaches student mediators alternative strategies to assist their peers in settling disputes in a manner that satisfies all parties. The philosophy supporting peer mediation programs is based upon these main premises:

1. Conflict is a disagreement or problem between two or more people.
2. Conflict is natural and inevitable in a social setting.

3. Individuals in conflict prefer to find peaceful solutions to problems.
4. Students can be responsible people who solve their own problems.

Peer Mediation Models

Peer mediation programs have been proven to be effective means in changing the way students understand and resolve conflict in their lives. There are three basic peer mediation models that are being used in schools around the nation:

1. In a *school-wide program*, students representing various grade levels and groups are chosen to participate in training. Those who successfully complete the course serve as school-wide peer mediators for a year. The mediations are scheduled and conducted in designated areas, such as on the playground before school and during lunch, during recess, and so forth. This is accomplished with minimal adult supervision. Mediators work on a team of two partners.
2. A *classroom model* involves the children in one or more grades who are all trained in conflict resolution skills. In addition, several students are selected to receive additional special peer mediation training. Those students serve as peer mediators in their own class or in other classes at their grade level or with younger children. Mediators work on a team of two partners.
3. A *whole class model* provides every student in a classroom with training in peer mediation skills. When two students are in disagreement about a solution to a problem, other students facilitate the mediation. Mediators work on a team of two partners.

A Description of the Program

When two students cannot decide on a reasonable solution to a problem, other students working in pairs assist by facilitating mediation at a "peace table" located in the classroom. Students in classrooms with effective peer mediation programs learn that there are alternatives to anger and violence for solving personal problems and interpersonal conflicts. Peer mediators do not "make decisions" but, rather, work toward a win-win resolution for both parties to avoid further confrontations. Peer mediators may deal with the following types of problems:

- Social improprieties
- Relationship problems
- Rumors and gossip
- Cheating
- Taking personal property without permission
- Minor racial and cultural confrontations
- Classroom and/or extracurricular disputes
- Minor bullying
- Minor assaults and arguments

More serious problems require a teacher intervention or a professional referral to the school counselor or other authorities and are not appropriate for peer mediation. These include situations such as sexual abuse, suicide threats, drug use, weapon possession, acts of violence, and anything of an illegal or immoral nature. There are numerous benefits that result from having an effective peer mediation program:

- Students learn *peaceful means to solve problems.*
- Students learn to *resolve their own problems* and *be responsible for their own actions.*
- Students improve *communication skills.*
- Students improve *problem-solving skills.*
- Students develop *confidence in the ability to help themselves.*
- Students learn that peers can *work together* to improve their school community.
- Peer mediators learn to *be responsible,* such as to be at work on time when a specific time is designated for the mediation or when they are assigned to playground duty; they also learn to follow the policies of the program.
- Peer mediators learn to be *positive leaders* and to set an example for other students.
- Statistics show that *levels of physical violence and verbal insults decrease* substantially in schools where there is a peer mediation program.

Implementing the Program

A common peer mediation program used in many classrooms trains all of the students in a classroom in mediation skills but chooses three teams of two partners to be the "Class Peer Mediators." It works well to have a girl-girl team, a boy-boy team, and a girl-boy team to facilitate the various issues students have.

When implementing a peer mediation program, allow students to apply for the position as you would apply for a job. Provide them with a copy of "The Qualities of a Good Peer Mediator" and have them write why they think they should be considered for the position (see the next section for a list of the *qualities of a good peer mediator*).

The teacher may select students for the position, but it is preferable to have the class vote on who they want as peer mediators to help them with their problems with other students. Once the peer mediators have been selected, parent permission forms must be sent home and signed. They must be returned before the training sessions begin.

Peer Mediation Training Sessions

The following program for the Peer Mediation Training Sessions has been adapted from the *Peer Mediation Elementary Curriculum Manual* (1998) as part of the Neighborhood Justice Center Project, Clark County Social Services, Las Vegas, Nevada.

A. Students will learn the *philosophy* of the peer mediation program.

1. Conflict is a disagreement or problem between two or more people.
2. Conflict is natural and inevitable in a social setting.
3. Individuals in conflict prefer to find peaceful solutions to problems.
4. Students can be responsible people who solve their own problems.

B. Students will learn the *qualities of a good peer mediator*.

1. Other students respect them.
2. They exhibit good verbal and listening skills.
3. They show leadership potential.
4. They show a willingness to try new things.
5. They work well on teams.
6. They show responsibility and commitment to the program.
7. They are positive role models.

8. They agree to make up any schoolwork missed as a result of mediation activities.
9. They have a strong desire to be a peer mediator.
10. They agree to attend all monthly peer mediation meetings.

C. Students will become aware of the *benefits* of the peer mediation program.

1. Students learn peaceful means to solve problems.
2. Students learn to resolve their own problems and be responsible for their own actions.
3. Students improve communication skills.
4. Students improve problem-solving skills.
5. Students develop confidence in the ability to help themselves.
6. Students learn to work with a partner.
7. Students learn that peers can work together to improve their school community.
8. Peer mediators learn responsibility—to be at work on time (if a specific time is designated for the mediation), to follow the policies of the program, and so on.
9. Peer mediators learn to be positive leaders—to set an example for other students.
10. Statistics show that levels of physical violence and verbal insults decrease substantially in schools where there is a peer mediation program.

D. Students will learn new *communication skills*.

1. Students will learn to express feelings using "I Messages":
   - I feel/felt _____ when you _____ because _____. I need you to _____. Or, Would you be willing to _____?
2. Students will become familiar with *facial expressions, tone of voice,* and *other body language cues* and what they mean.
3. Students will learn *active listening skills.*
   - Maintain eye contact when someone is speaking to you.
   - Do not interrupt the speaker.
   - Stand or sit still while the speaker is talking.

- Nod your head to show that you are understanding and interested in what the speaker is saying.
- Lean slightly toward the speaker when he or she is talking to you.
- After the speaker is finished talking, ask questions for clarification or respond appropriately to what the speaker has related to you.

E. Students will learn peer mediation *guidelines*, which must be followed.

1. Peer mediation is voluntary, so all disputants (individuals seeking help with their dispute) have to agree they want help to resolve the conflict.
2. Mediation should take place in a private setting, away from other peers (such as at a "peace table" or in a corner of the playground).
3. Mediators do not break up fights or intervene in any kind of violent behavior.
4. Mediators do not get involved in disputes that involve illegal or immoral acts.
5. Mediators must report any sign of illegal activity, threat of violence, or threat of suicide to the teacher.
6. Mediators always work in pairs.
7. Mediators always begin the mediation with the disputant who is most upset.
8. Mediators will fill out an agreement form on each mediation *when it occurs*.
9. Mediators will not discuss their mediations with any other students. They will keep the information shared with them *confidential*.

F. Students will learn the *processes* involved in being a peer mediator.

1. *Self-Introduction* by both mediators to make sure disputants know their names.

    Make sure both disputants agree to the *Ground Rules*:
    - No interrupting.
    - No name calling or put-downs.
    - Agree to work on resolving the conflict.

    The first disputant, the one who is most upset, tells his/her side of the story using "I Messages":

- I feel/felt _____ when _____ because _____.

The second disputant *restates* what the problem is for the other disputant. After restating, he/she may *ask questions* to better understand the problem.

- So, you felt _____ when _____ because _____.

2. Steps 3 and 4 are repeated with the second disputant telling his/her story using "I Messages" and the first disputant restating what he/she says.
3. Beginning with the first disputant, ask each person for *possible solutions* and take notes on the *Agreement Form*. In other words, have both disputants brainstorm possible solutions.
4. *Both agree on a solution* to the conflict and sign the Agreement Form. If a solution is not agreed upon, one of the mediators refers back to the list of possible solutions to find another one the disputants can agree upon.

The following guide may be used when making the Agreement Form:

The Agreement Form

First Mediator: First Disputant:
Second Mediator: Second Disputant:

GROUND RULES

- No interrupting.
- No name calling or put-downs.
- Agree to work on resolving the conflict.

First Disputant's Story: I feel/felt _____ when _____ because _____.

Notes:

Second Disputant restated the problem_____ (Yes or No)

SOLUTIONS TO THE CONFLICT

1.
2.
3.

Second Disputant's Story: I feel/felt _____ when _____ because _____.

Notes:

First Disputant restated the problem_____ (Yes or No)

SOLUTIONS TO THE CONFLICT

1.
2.
3.

THE SOLUTION AGREED UPON:

_____

SIGNATURES OF AGREEMENT:

First Disputant: Second Disputant:
Date of Mediation:

In summary, in a classroom peer mediation program, students act as conflict managers. They are taught a process of communication and problem solving that they apply to help their peers reach settlements of their conflicts without confrontation or violence. In the process of training, mediators learn, first, that conflicts can be constructive and positive and, second, that their role as mediators is not to judge (nor to impose an agreement or solution) but, rather, to guide disputants to move from blaming each other to devising solutions acceptable to all parties.

REFERENCES AND RESOURCES

Albert, L. (1996a). *A teacher's guide to cooperative discipline* (Rev. ed.). Circle Pines, MN: American Guidance Service.

Albert, L. (1996b). *Cooperative discipline.* Circle Pines, MN: American Guidance Service.

Allen, J. (1986). Classroom management: Students' perspectives, goals, and strategies. *American Educational Research Journal, 23,* 437–459.

Bear, G., Cavalier, A., and Manning, M. (2005). *Developing self-discipline and preventing and correcting misbehaviour.* Boston: Allyn & Bacon.

Charles, C. M. (2013). *Building classroom discipline* (11th ed.). New York: Pearson.

Dreikurs, R., and Cassel, P. (1972). *Discipline without tears.* New York: Hawthorn.

Glasser, W. (1999). *Choice theory: A new psychology of personal freedom.* New York: HarperCollins.

Kohn, A. (1996). *Beyond discipline: From compliance to community.* Alexandria, VA: Association for Supervision and Curriculum Development.

Kohn, A. (2001). *Beyond discipline: From compliance to community.* Upper Saddle River, NJ: Merrill / Prentice Hall.

Marshall, M. (2001). *Discipline without stress, punishments or rewards.* Los Alamitos, CA: Piper Press.

Marshall, M. (2005). Promoting positivity, choice and reflection. Retrieved from www.MarvinMarshall.com/promoting_positivity.htm.

Neighborhood Justice Center Project. (1998). *Peer mediation elementary curriculum manual.* Las Vegas, NV: Clark County Social Services.

Nelsen, J., Lott, L., and Glenn, H. (1997). *Positive discipline in the classroom.* Rocklin, CA: Prima.

Nelsen, J., Lott, L., and Glenn, H. (2000). *Positive discipline in the classroom: Developing mutual respect, cooperation, and responsibility in your classroom* (3rd ed.). Roseville, CA: Prima.

Styles, D. (2001). *Class meetings: Building leadership, problem-solving and decision-making skills in the respectful classroom.* Markham, ON: Pembroke Publishers.

Wolfgang, C. (2001). *Solving discipline and classroom management problems: Methods and models for today's teachers.* New York: John Wiley & Sons.

5

Building a Personal Democratic System of Discipline

Some Strategies, Theories, and Principles to Consider

It is important to create not only a warm, caring environment in which children can grow, develop, learn, and achieve but also a climate in which happy, self-confident, self-determining, and self-managing kids can flourish and thrive!

In this chapter, various discipline strategies, principles, and theories of behavior are presented for your consideration as you build or rebuild your own personal system of discipline conducive to and compatible with living in a democratic society. These strategies are designed to *prevent* misbehaviors before they happen, to teach kids how to behave responsibly, and to keep the school and home environments safe and conducive to nurturing and training healthy, happy, and successful kids.

To be effective, systems of discipline must meet the personal, social, and intellectual needs of the children involved, as well as address the needs of you, as educators and parents, as you assume your roles as democratic leaders for our children. For example, if you have an especially strong need for order, be up front about it and be willing to ask for your young people's cooperation and input.

A system of discipline includes the Code of Conduct, consequences for violation of the Code, and behavioral principles appropriate to the maintenance of order. More and more parents and educators are beginning to seriously consider discipline strategies to promote and encourage positive behaviors in children by methods other than punishment and intimidation.

For the discussion of various discipline strategies conducive to and compatible with living in a democratic society, the resource *Building Classroom Discipline* has been heavily relied upon with permission from the author, C. M. Charles. Dr. Charles is a leading expert and world-renowned authority in the area of classroom discipline. For more in-depth study of these and other discipline strategies, his works on the subject are strongly recommended.

Although Dr. Charles's books have provided an invaluable guide for providing a smorgasbord of various discipline strategies and behavior theories and principles, the original works of the authors who developed them have been consulted whenever possible.

Even though these strategies, behavior theories, and principles are based on classroom discipline models, they are easily transferrable to the home setting. They are intended for parents and guardians to consider when building their home systems of discipline. What applies to the classroom, when it comes to kids, applies to the home as well. Understanding these behavior theories and principles will also empower parents and guardians to help their children who might be having difficulties at school.

As democratic leaders, parents and educators assist their children in becoming respectful, caring, and empathetic toward others, responsible for the decisions that affect their lives, and effective in their practice of self-control, persistence, and self-discipline, in both the home and school environments. Is it important to create not only a warm, caring environment in which children can grow, develop, learn, and achieve but also a climate in which happy, self-confident, self-determining, and self-managing kids can flourish and thrive!

CHOICE THEORY: WILLIAM GLASSER

At least half of today's students will not commit themselves to learning if they find their school experience boring, frustrating, or otherwise dissatisfying.

—*William Glasser*

Discussion

William Glasser received early acclaim in the 1960s for his psychotherapy model of "Reality Therapy," which shifted the focus in treating problems in people's lives from childhood events to present realities. Shortly after writing his book on Reality Therapy, he applied his ideas to schooling. Choice Theory focuses on meeting students' basic needs as the primary means of ensuring class participation and desirable behavior. Glasser's contributions to classroom discipline include the following tenets:

- Application of his Choice Theory to the classroom.
- The focus on meeting students' basic needs.
- The concept of classroom meetings.
- The concepts and practices of quality curriculum, quality teaching, and quality learning.

In this section, the concepts of students' basic needs, Choice Theory, quality teaching, the seven deadly habits, and the seven connecting habits are discussed.

Students' Basic Needs

Glasser asserts that most classroom misbehavior occurs when students are bored or frustrated by class expectations, conditions that occur when students' basic needs are not being met. All students have five basic needs that must be met in order for them to flourish:

1. *Survival*—food, shelter, freedom from harm
2. *Belonging*—security, comfort, legitimate membership in the group
3. *Power*—sense of importance, of being significant to others
4. *Fun*—having a good time emotionally and intellectually
5. *Freedom*—to make choices and to exercise self-direction and responsibility

Glasser is so adamant about the importance of meeting all these basic student needs that he asserts that schools that do not meet these needs are bound to fail.

Choice Theory Principles

When students like the subject matter being studied—thus motivating them to want to learn more about it—they almost always do well and rarely misbehave. Choice Theory acknowledges that we cannot control anyone's behavior but our own, and we cannot *make* a student do anything. Glasser's principal teachings include these tenets:

- All our behavior is our best attempt to control ourselves and to meet the five basic needs.
- Students feel pleasure when their basic needs are met and frustration when they are not.
- At least half of today's students will not commit themselves to learning if they find their school experience boring, frustrating, or otherwise dissatisfying.
- Few students in today's schools do their best work.
- Curriculum and instruction must be aimed at meeting the basic needs.
- Student involvement and responsible behavior come from teachers helping students envision a quality existence in school and planning the choices that lead to it.
- What schools require is a commitment to quality education: this means quality curriculum and quality teaching that meet the five basic needs of students, as well as quality learning where students are involved, motivated, and responsible.

Quality Teaching

Quality teaching is as important as quality curriculum because it leads to quality learning. Teachers can achieve this status by providing the following to their students:

- *A warm, supportive classroom climate.* Let students know what you will and will not do for them. Demonstrate that you are always willing to help.
- *"Lead teaching" rather than "boss teaching."* Use methods that encourage and stimulate students. Don't try and force information into them.
- *Schoolwork that is useful.* The focus is on knowledge and skills that are useful in students' lives. At times, you may have to point out the value of new learning, or students will not make a sustained effort to learn.
- *Encouragement for students to do the best they can.* The process of doing quality work develops slowly and must be nurtured. Discuss quality work enough so students understand what you mean.

- *Opportunity for students to evaluate work they have done and improve it.* Quality is usually achieved by means of modifications to the work through continued effort.

Seven Deadly Habits and Seven Connecting Habits

From time to time, teachers can be seen using what Glasser refers to as *seven deadly habits* in trying to control student behavior. These habits are called "deadly" because they damage caring relationships with students. The deadly habits are criticizing, blaming, complaining, nagging, threatening, punishing, and rewarding. To maintain a positive relationship with your students and gain their enthusiastic cooperation, you must refrain from using the deadly habits and replace them with tactics that increase a sense of *connection* with students.

The *seven connecting habits* that nurture positive relationships with students are caring, listening, supporting, contributing, encouraging, trusting, and befriending. Glasser believes that all students can do competent work, provided teachers connect strongly with them.

References and Resources

Glasser, W. (1998a). *Choice theory in the classroom.* New York: HarperCollins.

Glasser, W. (1998b). *The quality school: Managing students without coercion.* New York: HarperCollins.

Glasser, W. (1998c). *The quality school teacher.* New York: HarperCollins.

Glasser, W. (1999). *Choice theory: A new psychology of personal freedom.* New York: HarperCollins.

Glasser, W. (2001). *Every student can succeed.* Chatsworth, CA: William Glasser.

DISCIPLINE WITH DIGNITY: RICHARD CURWIN AND ALLEN MENDLER

Responsibility is more important than obedience.

—*Richard Curwin and Allen Mendler*

Discussion

Dignity refers to respect for life and self. Kids with chronic behavior problems see themselves as losers and have stopped trying to gain acceptance through appropriate means, telling themselves it is better not to try than to fail yet again. They feel that their personal dignity is constantly under threat. They have little belief that they will ever be successful in school, or even that school has anything of value for them. However, most of these students can be rescued through tactics that boost their dignity and provide a sense of hope for success in school.

The Four-Phase Plan for Schools and Educators

Curwin and Mendler suggest a four-phase plan to help students move toward values-guided behavior:

1. *Identify the core values.* Teachers, school staff, students, and parents work together to identify a set of core values that shows how they want individuals in the class or school to conduct themselves and relate to each other. A set of core values might include the following statements:
   - School is a place where we solve our problems peacefully.
   - School is a place where we protect and look out for one another, rather than hurt or attack one another.
   - School is a place where we learn we are responsible for what we say and do.
   - School is a place where we learn "my way is not the only way."
2. *Create rules and consequences.* Rules are needed to govern classroom behavior and should be based on the school's stated values. For example:
   - Value: School is a place where we protect and look out for one another rather than hurt or attack one another.
   - Rule: No put-downs are allowed.
3. *Model the values.* It is essential that teachers and administrators continually model behaviors that are in keeping with the school values. Teachers must express their emotions nonviolently, use positive strategies to resolve conflicts with students, and walk away when they receive put-downs from students. In other words, teachers and administrators must "practice what they preach."
4. *Use no interventions that violate core values.* Teachers tend to use their past experiences when responding to student misbehavior. Their responses often take the form of threats, intimidation, and making examples of stu-

dents. Responses like these fail to model behavior consistent with school values and tend to produce further conflict.

Putting "Discipline with Dignity" into Practice

If you should have several chronically misbehaving students, and you feel Curwin and Mendler's model can help you work with them, you might base your efforts on the following four principles:

1. *Student dignity must always be preserved.* When faced with threat, students, especially those who chronically misbehave, use antisocial behavior to counter it.
2. *Dealing with misbehavior is one of the most important parts of teaching.* Find ways to encourage prosocial behavior.
3. *Lasting results are achieved only over time.* There are no quick-fix solutions to chronic misbehavior, but by finding ways to motivate students and help them learn, you will enable many to make genuine improvement.
4. *Responsibility is more important than obedience.* Put students into situations where they can make decisions about matters that concern them; be willing to allow them to fail and then help them try again. They will learn to behave in ways that are best for themselves and others.

References and Resources

Curwin, R. (1992). *Rediscovering hope: Our greatest teaching strategy.* Bloomington, IN: National Educational Service.

Curwin, R. (1995). A human approach to reducing violence in schools. *Educational Leadership, 52*(5), 72–75.

Curwin, R., and Mendler, A. (1988). *Discipline with dignity.* Alexandria, VA: Association for Supervision and Curriculum Development.

COOPERATIVE DISCIPLINE: LINDA ALBERT

For kids to meet their need for belonging in the class, they must come to see themselves as important, worthwhile, and valued as class members.

—Linda Albert

Discussion

Albert's fundamental hypothesis is that discipline occurs best when teachers and students work together in a genuinely cooperative manner to (1) establish a classroom that is safe, orderly, and inviting; (2) provide students a sense of connectedness and belonging; and (3) turn all behavior mistakes into opportunities for learning.

Genuine and Mistaken Goals and Consequent Behaviors

For kids to meet their need for belonging in the class, they must come to see themselves as important, worthwhile, and valued as class members. When they are unable to achieve a *sense of belonging*, the *genuine goal*, students often misbehave by pursuing *mistaken goals*. These mistaken goals are typically the following:

1. *Attention* (Look at me.)
2. *Power* (You can't make me.)
3. *Revenge* (I'll get even.)
4. *Withdrawal* (I won't participate.)

These mistaken goals correspond to the four types of classroom misbehavior as they seek in vain to gain a sense of belonging:

1. *Attention-Seeking Behavior.* When students do not get the attention they desire, they often seek it actively and passively. *Active* attention seeking includes behaviors such as pencil tapping, showing off, calling out, and asking irrelevant questions. *Passive* attention seeking involves behaviors such as dawdling, lagging behind, and slowness in complying.
2. *Power-Seeking Behavior.* Through action and words, students try to show that they cannot be controlled by the teacher.
3. *Revenge-Seeking Behavior.* When students get their feelings hurt, some may set out to retaliate against the teacher and/or classmates. This often happens when the teacher deals forcefully with a student, perhaps embarrassing him in front of his peers. This type of behavior often takes the form of a verbal attack, such as, *You really suck as a teacher!* It can also involve destruction of materials or damage to the physical environment.
4. *Avoidance-of-Failure Behavior.* Some students fear failure so greatly they give up and stop trying, preferring to appear lazy rather than stupid. You

might counter withdrawal by encouraging students to take one step at a time so they can have small successes. Another suggestion is to use hands-on activities for these children.

The Three C's of Cooperation

Fundamental to Albert's cooperative discipline are the *Three C's* of Cooperation, which help students see themselves as *capable* of experiencing success, *connected* with others, and *contributing* members of the class.

1. *Capable.* This is what Albert calls students' "I-can" level, meaning the belief they are capable of accomplishing the work given to them in school. She says teachers can increase students' sense of capability by (1) countering fear of mistakes, which keeps some students from trying; (2) building confidence that success is possible; (3) making progress tangible by having students compile albums and portfolios that display their accomplishments; and (4) recognizing achievement by having students acknowledge each other's accomplishments.
2. *Connected.* Albert advocates emphasizing the *Five A's* of Connecting: (1) *acceptance*—it's all right to be you; (2) *attention*—sharing your time and energy; (3) *appreciation*—positive acknowledgment of accomplishments; (4) *affirmation*—recognizing acts of courage, cheerfulness, dedication, kindness, and so on; and (5) *affection*—showing closeness and caring.
3. *Contributing.* There is a strong need for children to feel needed and valued, and one of the best ways to do this is to help them contribute to the class. Teachers can increase students' sense of contributing by doing the following: (1) encourage student input in class matters, (2) encourage student contributions to the school, (3) encourage student contributions to the community, (4) encourage students to work to protect the environment, and (5) encourage students to help other students.

References and Resources

Albert, L. (1984). *Coping with kids and school: A guide for parents.* New York: E. P. Dutton.

Albert, L. (1996a). *A teacher's guide to cooperative discipline* (Rev. ed.). Circle Pines, MN: American Guidance Service.

Albert, L. (1996b). *Cooperative discipline.* Circle Pines, MN: American Guidance Service.

Albert, L. (1996c). *Cooperative discipline: How to manage your classroom and promote self-esteem.* Circle Pines, MN: American Guidance Service.

INNER DISCIPLINE: BARBARA COLOROSO

Teachers must treat students as they, themselves, want to be treated.

—*Barbara Coloroso*

Discussion

The focus of Coloroso's work is treating students with respect—giving them the power and responsibility to make decisions. Discipline works best when teachers help students acquire an inner sense of self-control, which is developed through earning trust, assuming responsibility, and acquiring the power to make decisions. Discipline should be thought of as a means of teaching students to take positive control of their lives. The role of teachers is to provide guidance and support to help students manage their own discipline. *Teachers must treat students as they, themselves, want to be treated.*

How Punishment Differs from Discipline

Coloroso describes punishment as treatment that is psychologically hurtful to students and likely to provoke anger, resentment, and additional conflict. Students typically respond to punishment with the *Three F's*: fear, fighting back, or fleeing. Punishment impedes the development of integrity, wisdom, compassion, and mercy—all of which contribute to inner discipline.

In contrast, proper discipline leads students toward positive behavior by (1) showing them what they did wrong, (2) giving them ownership of the problems involved, (3) providing them strategies for solving the problems, and (4) leaving their dignity intact. Discipline, unlike punishment, helps students learn how to handle problems they will encounter throughout their lives, as well as in the present.

How to Deal with Misbehavior

According to Coloroso's theory, all misbehaviors fall into three categories: mistakes, mischief, and mayhem. *Mistakes* are errors that provide opportunity for learning better choices. *Mischief,* although not always serious, is intentional misbehavior. It provides an opportunity to help students find ways to fix what they did wrong and learn how to avoid repeating the behavior. *Mayhem,* which is willfully serious misbehavior, calls for application of the *Three R's of Reconciliatory Justice*:

1. *Restitution.* This means doing whatever is necessary to repair the damage that occurred.
2. *Resolution.* This denotes identifying and correcting whatever caused the misbehavior so it will not happen again.
3. *Reconciliation.* This involves healing relationships with people who were hurt by the misbehavior.

In all cases, students are allowed to experience the natural discomfort associated with the misbehavior and to make decisions and grow from the results. The main caution is to make sure student decisions do not lead to situations that are physically dangerous, morally threatening, or unhealthy. Otherwise, encourage students to face situations that require decisions, without making judgments, and allow them to proceed through the process. For example, *I see you have a problem. What is your plan for dealing with it?* You may need to provide guidance, but it will produce rapid growth in the ability to solve problems. Mistakes and poor choices become the students' responsibility.

References and Resources

Coloroso, B. (1994). *Kids are worth it! Giving your child the gift of inner discipline.* New York: William Morrow.

Coloroso, B. (2003). *The bully, the bullied, and the bystander: From preschool to high school—how parents and teachers can break the cycle of violence.* New York: HarperResource.

POSITIVE DISCIPLINE: JANE NELSEN AND LINDA LOTT

This climate allows students to behave with dignity, self-control, and concern for others.

—*Jane Nelsen and Linda Lott*

Discussion

Nelsen and Lott contend that discipline occurs best when teachers provide classroom climates that are accepting, encouraging, respectful, and supportive. This climate allows students to behave with dignity, self-control, and concern for others. The key to fostering this development is providing the structure that allows students to see themselves as capable, significant, and able to control their own lives.

Relationship Barriers and Relationship Builders

Nelsen and Lott identify five pairs of contrasting teacher behaviors they call barriers and builders. *Barriers* prevent good relationships because they are disrespectful and discouraging, whereas *builders* foster good relationships because they are respectful and encouraging. The following are some examples:

1. *Assuming versus Checking.* Rather than *assuming* you as teachers know what students think and feel, what they can or cannot do, or how they should or should not respond, it is better that you *check* with them.
2. *Rescuing/Explaining versus Exploring.* Rather than making lengthy explanations or rescuing students from difficulties, allow students to explore and perceive situations for themselves and to proceed on the basis of those perceptions.
3. *Directing versus Inviting/Encouraging.* Many teachers do not realize they are being disrespectful when they *direct* students with statements like *Pick that up, Put that away,* or *Clean off your desk.* Such commands build dependency and suppress initiate and cooperation. Teachers might say instead, *The bell is about to ring. I would appreciate anything you can do to get the room straightened up before we leave.*
4. *Expecting versus Celebrating.* Teachers should hold high expectations of students and believe in their potential. Students become easily discouraged if they are judged negatively when they fall short of expectations, such as in the comment, *I thought you were more responsible than that.* Students respond far better when teachers look for improvements and call attention to them.

The Role of Classroom Meetings

Nelsen and Lott believe classroom meetings are uniquely suited for implementing their strategies to build positive discipline. These meetings promote social skills such as listening, taking turns, hearing different points of view, negotiating, communicating, helping one another, and taking responsibility for one's own behavior. Academic skills are enhanced as well because students must practice language skills, attentiveness, critical thinking, decision making, and problem solving.

When teachers involve themselves as partners with students in class meetings, it creates a climate of mutual respect and dignity. Teachers and students listen to one another, take each other seriously, and work together to solve problems for the benefit of all.

References and Resources

Nelsen, J., Lott, L., and Glenn, H. (1997). *Positive discipline in the classroom.* Rocklin, CA: Prima.

Nelsen, J., Lott, L., and Glenn, H. (2000). *Positive discipline in the classroom: Developing mutual respect, cooperation, and responsibility in your classroom* (3rd ed.). Roseville, CA: Prima.

THE SYNERGETIC CLASSROOM: C. M. CHARLES

Students get caught up in group spirit and a strong sense of purpose.

—*C. M. Charles*

Discussion

C. M. Charles, a renowned leading expert in classroom discipline, defines the term *synergy* as a phenomenon in which two or more people interact in a manner that builds mutual energy. He asserts that *synergy* can play an important role in making classroom discipline more effective and pleasant for everyone. Charles contends that discipline programs are most effective when they (1) make provisions for meeting student needs, (2) emphasize conditions and activities that students find attractive, (3) eliminate or minimize conditions and activities that students generally dislike, and (4) foster ethics and trust among members of the class.

Synergy and Synergetic Discipline

Synergetic discipline is the behavior management portion of *synergetic teaching*, a way of teaching and working with students that produces quality learning and responsible behavior, while removing much of the job stress teachers normally experience. Charles believes that good classroom behavior is best established by teachers and students cooperating to meet individuals' needs in the classroom, to minimize the causes of misbehavior, and, when appropriate, to energize the class for greater enjoyment and easier learning.

In the classroom, this synergetic condition typically leads to increased productivity, creativity, satisfaction, and enjoyment. Students get caught up in group spirit and a strong sense of purpose. Teachers report that, during episodes of synergy, discipline problems are largely nonexistent.

Implementing Synergetic Teaching

The following is Charles's description of how to implement synergetic teaching and discipline in the classroom (2008, p. 246):

1. Invite your students sincerely to work with you in maintaining an interesting, inviting program for learning, one that is free from fear and based on personal dignity and consideration for others.
2. Involve students in discussing the details of your discipline plan and listen to suggestions they might have. Make sure they understand what it involves, what their responsibilities are, and what your responsibilities are.
3. Discuss and demonstrate conditions that build class spirit and energy. Continually ask the class to help identify topics and activities they find appealing.
4. Discuss student (and teacher) misbehavior, how it is manifested, why it is detrimental to learning, and the factors that are known to foster it. Elicit student ideas about how they can work with you to eliminate these factors.

Students' Basic Needs

Discuss with your class and take into account the basic needs we all share. Charles has relied on contributions from various others in the field of classroom discipline, and they include these tenets:

1. *Security*: A sense of safety without worry.
2. *Hope*: The belief that school is worthwhile and success is possible.
3. *Dignity*: Feeling respected and worthwhile.
4. *Belonging*: Feeling a part of things, being valued, and having a place in the class.

5. *Power*: Having some control of and input into events in the class.
6. *Enjoyment*: Finding pleasure in activities that are stimulating or rewarding.
7. *Competence*: Being able to do many things well, including the expected schoolwork.

Addressing Conflicts

Conflicts are interpersonal situations characterized by disagreements, which may or may not include misbehavior. Conflicts threaten personal dignity, which students strongly defend. Conflicts are best resolved through a *win-win approach* in which both sides feel most of their concerns are being properly addressed. The following suggestions are provided to *reduce conflicts* in the classroom:

1. Make sure all individuals involved have the opportunity to express their concerns.
2. Insist that all comments, observations, and suggestions are presented in a courteous manner.
3. Encourage both sides to be open and honest but also tactful.
4. Keep attention focused on areas of agreement between the disputants.
5. Help disputants formulate solutions as joint agreements.
6. Do not allow students to argue, defend themselves, or debate.

It is important to give students the tools to find peaceful solutions to avoid heated verbal and physical confrontations.

References and Resources

Charles, C. M. (2000). *The synergetic classroom*. Boston: Allyn & Bacon.

Charles, C. M. (2002). *Essential elements of effective discipline*. Boston: Allyn & Bacon.

Charles C. M. (2013). *Building classroom discipline* (11th ed.). New York: Pearson.

BUILDING YOUR OWN SYSTEM OF DISCIPLINE

Schools and homes should be democratic places for kids to learn, grow, and flourish.

What Is the Purpose of a System of Discipline?

This section is provided to assist pre-service teachers, seasoned teachers, and parents in formulating, building, or rebuilding their own system of discipline compatible with living in a democratic society. It provides teachers and parents with the tools to prepare discipline systems that (1) teach children how to behave responsibly, (2) teach children to cooperate, (3) teach children self-control and self-discipline, (4) teach children to make wise decisions and solve daily problems, (5) develop positive relationships, (6) develop good communication skills, and (7) keep classrooms and homes safe and conducive to nurturing and learning.

Effective discipline systems teach kids how to behave properly and, at the same time, provides for minimizing misbehavior. In order to be effective, your discipline system must meet the basic needs of your children, as well as your *own* needs. High-quality discipline systems in schools (although they may be applied to the home setting as well) give attention to the following concepts:

1. *Preventative Discipline:* Teachers (parents) make the curriculum (home activities) fun and enjoyable and teach and model good behavior.
2. *Supportive Discipline:* Teachers (parents) show interest in students (their children), provide help, and keep them on track.
3. *Corrective Discipline:* Teachers (parents) stop misbehavior, reteach correct behavior, and preserve dignity in the process.

Steps in Building a Discipline System

When children are involved in formulating the system of discipline, they are more likely to respect the behavioral goals, abide by the Code of Conduct, and be more willing to accept the consequences for failure to comply. The following steps provide structure for the process:

STEP 1: *Specify your role as the teacher/parent* with input from your children (a democratic leader? a guide? a supporter? a friend?). How will you conduct yourself? For example, treat others with respect, courtesy, and kindness.

STEP 2: *Identify the classroom/home behavioral goals* with your children. Clarify the social, emotional, and moral behavior children and teachers/parents need in order to interact respectfully with others. Examples: Have a positive attitude, be considerate of others, take initiative, show self-direction, and exhibit responsibility for your own actions.

STEP 3: Describe the *classroom/home conditions* you and your children want to create. Examples: sense of community, positive attention, good communication, consideration for others, trusting relationships, interesting activities, helping each other, and input from children in decisions that affect their lives.

STEP 4: Involve children in developing a *Class/Family Code of Conduct*. It may be useful to provide them with Albert's teacher-generated Code of Conduct (which can be applied to the home setting as well, especially the first four):

1. I am respectful.
2. I am responsible.
3. I am safe.
4. I am prepared.

Because "Excellence in Education" is our motto:

5. I will do nothing to prevent the teacher from teaching or prevent anyone, myself included, from participating in educational activities.
   I will cooperate with all members of the school community.
   I will treat everyone with respect and courtesy.

Then have your students identify appropriate and inappropriate behaviors for each principle. (Refer to chapter 4 for more details on drafting a Code of Conduct.)

STEP 5: With the assistance of your children, specify the *consequences for violations of the Code of Conduct*. (Refer to chapter 4 for more details on formulating the consequences.)

STEP 6: At school, *involve parents* by sending home a letter (or have students write the letter) explaining the class system of discipline and asking for their input and support.

STEP 7: Post a copy of the Class/Family Code of Conduct and review it with your children as needed. It can also be used for reference if a student is misbehaving. For example, if a student is making unkind comments about another student, on a small slip of paper you can write, "#1 of the C of C." (Code of Conduct), and the student would see, "I am respectful."

This type of discipline system will help provide an exciting learning environment where kids can achieve, succeed, and thrive, and where behavior problems will be minimized and gradually become insignificant.

Involve Kids in the Process

In order for our kids to feel stimulated and encouraged to voluntarily participate in the maintenance of order, they must feel included in the process of forming the rules, as well as the consequences for failure to comply. Kids must develop skills in self-control, self-discipline, cooperation, and making good decisions. By teaching and allowing kids to be responsible for their own decisions and actions, you give them a sense of empowerment and self-worth. They need to perceive themselves as capable, valued, and in control of their own lives.

Creating a Democratic Climate for Kids

Once a system is established where dignity, respect, and freedom to make choices is bestowed upon our kids, then the principles of responsibility, obligation, cooperation, and respect for order can be learned. Schools and homes must be democratic places for kids to learn, grow, succeed, and flourish. As you create a warm, caring, respectful climate of acceptance, dignity, and encouragement, your children will grow and develop into responsible, self-directing, and self-managing individuals, a gift that will last a lifetime!

References and Resources

Albert, L. (1996b). *Cooperative discipline.* Circle Pines, MN: American Guidance Service.

Charles, C. M. (2013). *Building classroom discipline* (11th ed.). New York: Pearson.

Appendix: A Quick Reference to Useful Tools to Promote Positive Behaviors

Excerpts from Encouraging Positive Behaviors in Today's Kids by Mary Lou McCormick

INDEX

Kids' Basic Needs
Linda Albert's Three C's for Belonging
Negative Ways to Get Recognition
A Plan for Solving Problems
SODAS, A Decision-Making Process
A Process for Setting Goals
Dealing with Anger/Aggression Issues
Helping Kids with Anger/Aggression Issues
Anger Analysis
Student Rights Regarding Bullying
Helping Kids Deal with Bullies
A Bullying / Harassment Survey

KIDS' BASIC NEEDS

According to Glasser (1992), children's basic needs must be met before the spark for learning can even be lit. These needs include (1) *survival*—food, shelter, and safety; (2) *belonging*—security, comfort, and group membership; (3) *power*—sense of importance and consideration by others; (4) *fun*—having a good time emotionally and intellectually; and (5) *freedom*—of choices and having self-direction and responsibility. If these needs are not met, children are not interested in going to school. It is as simple as that. The happier kids are at school, the more instilled they are with the desire to learn, and the more they feel they belong to the group. Increase children's sense of belonging by giving them specific tasks with a title that provides a service to the class group. Here are a few examples:

- The class attendance clerk (e.g., make an unofficial classroom attendance card and have the student mark the students present each morning)
- The chief boys/girls restroom monitor
- The class cafeteria captain
- The class distributor (passes out papers, supplies, and other things)

Frequently let children know how important their task is to the group.

LINDA ALBERT'S THREE C'S FOR BELONGING

Albert (1996c) devised the *Three C's* of helping kids feel they belong:

1. *Capable* or "I-can" level—helping kids feel they are capable of learning, achieving, and succeeding.
2. *Connect*—assisting kids in initiating and maintaining positive relationships with peers and teachers by using the *Five A's* (acceptance, attention, appreciation, affirmation, and affection).
3. *Contribute*—making kids feel *needed* by the group by contributing to their class, their school, and their community, as well as helping out other students.

It is important to help kids feel secure about themselves, to help them to learn how to make positive decisions every day that affect their lives, and to be accountable for their own actions. This will serve as solid footing for making such decisions as *responsible school attendance* in the present and *reliable work ethics* in the future.

NEGATIVE WAYS TO GET RECOGNITION

The following is a description of the negative methods used to gain recognition and social status when acceptable means appear unavailable to the child:

- *Power*: If the adult gets into a power struggle with the child and wins, the child is only convinced of the value of power and is more determined to win next time.
- *Revenge*: Revenge is the result of antagonism and animosity. The child finds his place in the group by making himself disliked.
- *Inadequacy*: The child "expects" failure and uses inability and helplessness to escape positive participation.
- *Defiance*: Defiance is the refusal to abide by the rules that govern the group. A child would rather be punished than ignored.

These are attempts to foster the basic need that every child has—to belong to the group. In the school setting this youngster may take on the role of the class clown, the class bully, or the class jerk, but at least he feels like he *belongs* to the "class" group. In the home environment, a child might achieve his recognition, attention, and social status within the family by taking on the role of the family clown, the baby of the family, the family troublemaker, and so forth, in order to attain his sense of belonging to the "family" group.

A PLAN FOR SOLVING PROBLEMS

One of the most effective ways of developing self-control in kids is to teach them problem-solving strategies. Give children a variety of problematic scenarios and, using the problem-solving format that follows, have them practice resolving the issues.

1. Identify the problem. *In your own words, what is the problem?*
2. Determine the goal. *What do you want to happen?*
3. List the options. *What are some ways you could choose to deal with the problem?*
4. Choose one option. *Choose the way you think would be best.* When dealing with a real-life problem, they would include the following steps:
5. Carry out the plan.
6. Evaluate how successful the plan was in solving the problem and revise if necessary.

Children will learn there is no problem so great it cannot be solved.

SODAS: A DECISION-MAKING PROCESS

One decision-making process to teach kids self-control uses the acronym SODAS, which stands for situation, options, disadvantages, advantages, and solution. This activity can be used with an individual and with groups. The purpose is to teach children to reason out a situation and evaluate the advantages and disadvantages of choices before making a decision. Provide various problematic scenarios and allow children to practice resolving the issue.

1. Identify the *Situation. What exactly is the decision to be made? Be specific about the issue to be decided. Answer the "who, what, where when, and why" questions.* (Remind them to avoid being emotional, because emotion tends to cloud judgment.)
2. List all the *Options. What are the possible choices at hand? List both the good and bad options, even those that show out-of-control behavior.*
3. List the *Disadvantages* of each option given above. The idea is to get kids to see the negative consequences of an option.
4. List the *Advantages* of each option given earlier. By exploring both the advantages and disadvantages of an option, kids will be better prepared to see why an option might work or fail.
5. Choose a *Solution.* Give kids some time to think about the solutions, then allow them to make the choice as to which option might be the best. It may not be the choice you want, but this is part of the learning process. As long as the choice is not immoral or illegal, let them make the choice and deal with the consequences.

A PROCESS FOR SETTING GOALS

In order for children to learn how to set goals, they need a process to follow. Here are the steps involved in setting goals:

1. *Determine the Goal.* The goal should always be age appropriate and something the child really wants to achieve. We can encourage children to explore various ideas, but if the goal is not something your child really wants, the chances are she will give up before she even starts. Let's use as an example, a grade 4 student, Sarah, who just received her report card and is not happy with her grade in math. She has determined she wants to set a goal: To earn a better grade in math.

2. *Set up a Plan of Action.* As with the goal, the plan of action must also be age appropriate. The younger the child is the more simple the goal, the shorter the time frame, and the fewer the steps to achieve it. Sarah tells her teacher she wants to earn a better grade in math, and her teacher helps her set up a plan of action to achieve her goal:
   - Complete all seat work assignments.
   - Complete all homework assignments.
   - Study for tests and quizzes.
   - Participate in class.
   - Show attentive behavior in class.
   - Ask questions when confused.
   - Work well with others.
   - Work well independently.
3. *Measuring Success.* How to measure success is different for everyone, and different for every goal. In Sarah's case, her goal may be to raise her grade in math from a D to a C, or from a C to a B, or from a B to an A, depending on what grade she had received previously on her report card. The teacher could help her monitor her success by providing her with a weekly progress report on which the eight steps of her plan of action are listed. Sarah could keep a checklist of the steps on her desk to remind her of what needs to be done. Her teacher could check the steps of the plan that were completed successfully, as well as give her a grade for the week. At the end of the grading period, if Sarah has indeed achieved her goal and raised her grade in math, her teacher and parents should celebrate her success with her!

Most youngsters are interested in improving their social skills, and this is an excellent area in which to work cooperatively with kids to practice setting and achieving goals. Once the need for a goal is established, such as making new friends, for example, and various options for the plan of action have been devised by the class to achieve that goal, it is helpful to have students role play and model the various options to see what might work best for them.

DEALING WITH ANGER/AGGRESSION ISSUES

In an attempt to understand the child who exhibits these negative behaviors of anger and aggression, it may be helpful to consider the following scenarios:

- The child's parents and/or siblings use aggressive behavior to resolve conflicts at home, often ending in angry, abusive, and even violent disputes. These are the child's role models. He may adhere to the belief that aggressive acts are the only options available to him.
- The child experiences a sense of powerlessness in the home environment but discovers that there is power in angry, aggressive behavior at school and in the community.
- The child's home environment is chaotic, and family members are abusive toward each other and toward the child. The child carries his emotional pain to school. His way of coping with this emotional pain may be to create havoc at school by exhibiting aggressive behavior toward other students and/or the teacher, thus taking the focus of his mind off the pain inflicted upon him at home.
- The child receives more attention (albeit *negative* attention) when he displays aggressive, deviant behavior than when he is well behaved and compliant; thus, he chooses the behaviors that award him the most attention.
- The child has a reputation for being mean and aggressive—a fighter. The child internalizes these views others have of him and is simply living up to their expectations, as well as his own self-perceptions.
- The child frequently displays angry, and sometimes aggressive, behavior when confronted with tasks he considers to be too difficult for him. He would rather be perceived as mean or bad than dumb or stupid.
- All behavior has meaning and purpose within the child's social context. If the child lacks a *sense of belonging* within his social groups of home and school, he may lack confidence in himself to succeed by useful and positive means.

HELPING KIDS WITH ANGER/AGGRESSION ISSUES
The following are some suggestions to consider when helping children who are having difficulties with anger and aggression:

- Give children responsibilities to help them feel they are *connected* and *contributing* to the good of the group. Frequently let them know how important their tasks are to the group.
- Provide the child with opportunities for *social and academic successes* and give frequent, positive feedback that indicates he or she is important and respected.

- Assess that the *difficulty of a given task* is within the child's ability to perform successfully, given the allotted amount of time for completion.
- Provide the children with as many *high-interest and "fun" activities* within the academic setting, thus increasing their level of happiness and sense of well-being.
- Give children *choices* whenever possible. For example, *Here are two papers that need to be completed. Which one would you like to do first?* Or, *This assignment needs to be completed because it gives you practice in multiplication. Would you like to use the yellow pencil or my mechanical pencil?* (Kids love using mechanical pencils, so the child will probably choose it and get busy working on the assignment.)
- If necessary, provide a *quiet place* for the child to work independently, away from peer interactions. Include his opinion in determining where he might feel most comfortable. Allow him to rejoin the group during those times in which a quiet place is not necessary. Besides reducing frustrating distractions, this will lessen his need to "save face" if the task is difficult for him.

Self-control skills are among the most valuable tools that educators can help their kids develop. They are some of the most important skills for success—not only now when they are young but also throughout their lives.

ANGER ANALYSIS
Anger analysis involves analyzing the anger-provoking situation with the child.

1. Assist the child in *identifying the signs* that indicate anger, such as rapid heartbeat, shortness of breath, rapid breathing, face feels hot, hands clench up, stomach feels tight, and so on.
2. Have the child *identify the event* that happened *prior* to the angry feeling.
3. Encourage the child to *express his feelings* about the event by using the I Message format:
    - I feel/felt _____ when _____ because _____ and I need/want _____.
    - Example: I feel *angry* when *Carlos calls me Shorty* because *it embarrasses me in front of my friends*, and I want *him to stop*.

4. Discuss *alternative ways* to deal with situations that cause frustration and anger, for example, walking away, talking it out, taking "time out" to cool off, changing the game, counting to 30, and so forth.
5. Have the child choose *one alternative way* he could have responded to the current situation being discussed and have him role play the alternative choice.
6. If necessary and the child agrees, *formulate a behavior agreement*, based on the process of setting and achieving goals, and offer to assist him:
   - State the Goal—What do you want to happen?
   - The Plan of Action—What are the steps you will need to take in order to reach your goal?
   - Evaluation—How well did your plan work? Did you reach your goal? What changes *might you make for next time?*

STUDENT RIGHTS REGARDING BULLYING
Inform students of their *rights* regarding bullying:

1. You have the right to be treated with respect.
2. You have the right not to be teased.
3. You have the right to tell others to stop bothering you and have the request respected.
4. You have the right to complain and be taken seriously.
5. You have the right to make a report regarding the complaint and have it investigated.
6. You have the right to expect support from school authorities.

HELPING KIDS DEAL WITH BULLIES
Educators and parents must help their children become aware of the presence of bullying. With adult guidance, the kids need to devise a plan of action designed to avoid becoming victims of a bully. Included in the plan might be the following steps:

1. Try to ignore the bully. If that doesn't work, tell the bully in a firm voice, *Stop bothering me.*
2. Walk away from the bully and seek a safe place close to an adult or other kids.
3. Socialize and make friends.
4. Participate in activities in which you excel.

APPENDIX

5. If you see someone being bullied, seek the help of an adult or report the situation to the proper authorities.
6. If someone does bully you, find someone you trust and discuss the situation.

Build confidence by *role playing* ways to deal with a bully. Practice ignoring the bully, walking away from the situation, and being assertive (like firmly telling the bully, *Stop bothering me*).

A BULLYING/HARASSMENT SURVEY

A Bully/Harassment Survey should be conducted periodically throughout the school year. Children are not required to sign their names to the survey, and the information is confidential. If there are any questions they prefer not answering, tell them to leave it blank. Stress that this survey has no bearing on their grade in class. The surveys can be formatted for students to indicate a choice of one of the following: Always, Often, Sometimes, and Hardly Ever.

For Younger Children

What grade are you in?   Are you a girl or boy?

1. Has anyone ever called you a name?
2. Has anyone ever told you that you can't be friends?
3. Has anyone ever hit, kicked, or pushed you?
4. Has anyone ever threatened you?
5. Was someone mean to you because of how you look?
6. Did you tell anyone about any of these incidents? Why or why not?
7. Have you ever seen someone else being bullied?
8. Have you ever called someone else a name, or hit, kicked, pushed, threatened, or been mean to someone?

For Older Children

What grade are you in?   Are you a male or female?

1. Do you feel safe at school? Why, or why not?
2. Have you ever stayed home from school because you were afraid of being bullied?

3. Do you feel safe on your way to school and going back home? Why or why not?
4. Do you feel safe in your neighborhood?
5. Have you ever been bullied?
6. Is someone bullying you while you are on your way to school, at school, or on your way home? Who is it? (Your answer will be private.)
7. Have you seen someone else being bullied? Who was it? Who was doing the bullying?
8. Have you seen groups of kids making fun of, seriously teasing, or harassing someone? If so, who was the person being harassed?
9. Who were the students doing the harassing? (Remember, this is a private survey.)

During the past four weeks, have you been bullied or harassed by other students in any of the following ways?
- Physically?
- Verbally?
- Socially?
- Cyberbullying? (Texts, e-mail, Facebook, and so on)

During the past four weeks, have you experienced bullying or harassment in any of the following areas?
- Race, ethnic group, culture?
- Sexual?
- Gender? (Male or female issues)
- Religion?
- Disability?
- Homophobic, or lifestyle preference (such as gay bashing)?
- Economic status or income based?

REFERENCES AND RESOURCES

Albert, L. (1996c). *Cooperative discipline: How to manage your classroom and promote self-esteem.* Circle Pines, MN: American Guidance Services

Glasser, W. (1998b). *The quality school: Managing students without coercion.* New York: HarperCollins.

Bibliography

Adler, A. (2009). *Social interest: Adler's key to the meaning of life* (Reprint ed.). Oxford: OneWorld.

Albert, L. (1984). *Coping with kids and school: A guide for parents.* New York: E. P. Dutton.

Albert, L. (1989). *A teacher's guide to cooperative discipline: How to manage your classroom and promote self-esteem.* Circle Pines, MN: American Guidance Service.

Albert, L. (1996a). *A teacher's guide to cooperative discipline* (Rev. ed.). Circle Pines, MN: American Guidance Service.

Albert, L. (1996b). *Cooperative discipline.* Circle Pines, MN: American Guidance Service.

Albert, L. (1996c). *Cooperative discipline: How to manage your classroom and promote self-esteem.* Circle Pines, MN: American Guidance Service.

Allen, J. (1986). Classroom management: Students' perspectives, goals, and strategies. *American Educational Research Journal, 23,* 437–459.

Angell, A. (1991). Democratic climates in elementary classrooms: A review of theory and research. *Theory and Research in Social Education, 19,* 241–266.

Apple, M., and Beane, J. (Eds.). (1995). *Democratic schools.* Alexandria, VA: Association for Supervision and Curriculum Development.

Baumeister, R., and Leary, M. (1995). The need to belong: Desire for interpersonal attachments as a fundamental human motivation. *Psychological Bulletin, 117,* 497–529.

Bear, G., Cavalier, A., and Manning, M. (2005). *Developing self-discipline and preventing and correcting misbehaviour.* Boston: Allyn & Bacon.

Blake, S., Brady, T., and Sanchez, S. (2004). Enculturation of democratic principles in the young: A vision of equity education in public schools. *Educational Research Quarterly, 28*(1), 48–59.

Blum, D. (1998). *The school counselor's book of lists.* San Francisco, CA: Jossey-Bass.

Brockman, E. (1996). Removing the paradox of conflict from group dynamics. *Academy of Management Executive, 10*(2), 61–62.

Capozzoli, T. (1995). Resolving conflict within teams. *Journal for Quality and Participation, 8*(7), 28–30.

Centers for Disease Control and Prevention. (2018). School-associated student homicides—United States, 1992-2016. *Morbidity and Mortality Weekly Report, 57*(2), 33–36. Last reviewed October 24, 2019.

Centers for Disease Control and Prevention. (2018). Youth risk behavior surveillance—United States, Surveillance Summaries. Last reviewed August 22, 2019.

Charles, C. M. (1999). *Building classroom discipline* (6th ed.). New York: Longman.

Charles, C. M. (2000). *The synergetic classroom.* Boston: Allyn & Bacon.

Charles, C. M. (2002). *Essential elements of effective discipline.* Boston: Allyn & Bacon.

Charles C. M. (2008). *Building classroom discipline* (9th ed.). Boston: Allyn & Bacon.

Charles, C. M. (2013). *Building classroom discipline* (11th ed.). New York: Pearson.

Coloroso, B. (1994). *Kids are worth it! Giving your child the gift of inner discipline.* New York: William Morrow.

Coloroso, B. (2003). *The bully, the bullied, and the bystander: From preschool to high school—how parents and teachers can break the cycle of violence.* New York: HarperResource.

Corey, G. (2004). *Theory and practice of group counseling* (6th ed.). Monterey, CA: Brooks/Cole.

Cormier, W., and Cormier, L. (1979). *Interviewing strategies for helpers: A guide to assessment, treatment and evaluation.* Monterey, CA: Brooks/Cole.

Corsini, R. (2007). Corsini's individual education: A democratic model. Groups in educational settings [Special issue]. *Group Dynamics: Theory, Research, and Practice, 11*(4), 247–252.

Curwin, R. (1992). *Rediscovering hope: Our greatest teaching strategy.* Bloomington, IN: National Educational Service.

Curwin, R. (1995). A human approach to reducing violence in schools. *Educational Leadership, 52*(5), 72–75.

Curwin, R., and Mendler, A. (1988). *Discipline with dignity.* Alexandria, VA: Association for Supervision and Curriculum Development.

Deutch, M., and Coleman, P. (Eds.). (2000). *The handbook of conflict resolution: Theory and practice.* San Francisco, CA: Jossey-Bass.

Dinkmeyer, D., and Dreikurs, R. (1963). *Encouraging children to learn.* New York: Hawthorn Books.

Dreikurs, E. (2001). Adler and Dreikurs: Cognitive-social dynamic innovators. *Journal of Individual Psychology, 57*(4), 324–341.

Dreikurs, R. (1964). *Children: The challenge.* New York: Hawthorn/Dutton.

Dreikurs, R. (1968). *Psychology in the classroom* (2nd ed.). New York: Harper & Row.

Dreikurs, R. (2009). *Child guidance and education: Collected papers of Rudolf Dreikurs.* New York: Alfred Adler Institute.

Dreikurs, R., and Cassel, P. (1972). *Discipline without tears.* New York: Hawthorn.

Dreikurs, R., Grunwald, B., and Pepper, E. (1982). *Maintaining sanity in the classroom.* New York: Harper & Row.

Evans, D., Hearn, M., Uhlemann, M., and Ivey, A. (1979). *Essential interviewing: A programmed approach to effective communication.* Monterey, CA: Brooks/Cole.

Gibson, R., Mitchell, M., and Basile, S. (1993). *Counseling in the elementary classroom: A comprehensive approach.* Boston: Allyn & Bacon.

Glasser, W. (1998a). *Choice theory in the classroom.* New York: HarperCollins.

Glasser, W. (1998b). *The quality school: Managing students without coercion.* New York: HarperCollins.

Glasser, W. (1998c). *The quality school teacher.* New York: HarperCollins.

Glasser, W. (1999). *Choice theory: A new psychology of personal freedom.* New York: HarperCollins.

Glasser, W. (2001). *Every student can succeed.* Chatsworth, CA: William Glasser.

Gordon, T. (1989). *Discipline that works: Promoting self-discipline in children.* New York: Random House.

Hartnett, T. (2011). *Consensus-oriented decision making.* Gabriola Island, BC: New Society Publishers.

Hockenberry, S., and Puzzanchera, C. (2019). Juvenile court statistics 2017. *OJJD Fact Sheet.* Office of Juvenile Justice and Delinquency, U.S. Department of Justice. Retrieved from http://www.ncjj.org/pdf/jcsreports/jcs2017report.pdf.

Kohn, A. (1996). *Beyond discipline: From compliance to community.* Alexandria, VA: Association for Supervision and Curriculum Development.

Kohn, A. (2001). *Beyond discipline: From compliance to community.* Upper Saddle River, NJ: Merrill / Prentice Hall.

Loh, A. (2009). Teaching problem-solving skills to children—why are they so important? Retrieved from http://www.brainy-child.com/articles/teach-problem-solving-skills.shtml.

Malone, H. (2008). Civic education in America's public schools: Developing service-and-politically-oriented youth. *Phi Kappa Phi Forum, 88*(2), 24.

Marshall, M. (2001). *Discipline without stress, punishments or rewards.* Los Alamitos, CA: Piper Press.

Marshall, M. (2005). Promoting positivity, choice and reflection. Retrieved from www.MarvinMarshall.com/promoting_positivity.htm.

Neighborhood Justice Center Project. (1998). *Peer mediation elementary curriculum manual.* Las Vegas, NV: Clark County Social Services.

Nelsen, J., Lott, L., and Glenn, H. (1997). *Positive discipline in the classroom.* Rocklin, CA: Prima.

Nelsen, J., Lott, L., and Glenn, H. (2000). *Positive discipline in the classroom: Developing mutual respect, cooperation, and responsibility in your classroom* (3rd ed.). Roseville, CA: Prima.

Rogers, C. (1961). *On becoming a person.* Boston: Houghton Mifflin.

Styles, D. (2001). *Class meetings: Building leadership, problem-solving and decision-making skills in the respectful classroom.* Markham, ON: Pembroke Publishers.

Wolfgang, C. (2001). *Solving discipline and classroom management problems: Methods and models for today's teachers.* New York: John Wiley & Sons.

About the Author

Mary Lou McCormick is a licensed professional guidance counselor who has made it her life-long career working with young people in "at-risk" schools in Texas, New Mexico, and Nevada. Along with her regular duties as a school guidance counselor in Las Vegas, she served as a Clark County school district crisis counselor for all grade levels for many years. She earned a master's degree in education from West Texas A&M and pursued graduate studies in psychological and educational counseling at Texas Tech University. As a former elementary and secondary school teacher, she first realized many of today's youth are in serious trouble. As she relays, "Without new methods and strategies compatible with democratic principles for raising and training today's kids . . . the incidence of maladjustment, deficiency, and outright rebellion and violence found among many of today's kids will most likely continue to rise."

Lightning Source UK Ltd.
Milton Keynes UK
UKHW010236250920
370476UK00001B/32